Giving a $#!+

How a Willingness to Be Inconvenienced Can
Transform Your Business, Work, and Life

NEAL WOODSON

Contents

GIVING A $#!+

Foreword

I was the keynote speaker at a local school's Veteran's Day program this year, and the title of my speech was "The Value of Service." I told the students, faculty, and gathered guests that veterans served their fellow Americans by being willing to fight to protect them. This willingness to serve others is why people often say to veterans, "Thank you for your service."

There are 16.2 million veterans in the United States, which represents only five percent of all Americans. Veterans represent a small group of Americans willing to serve to protect everyone else.

The question to consider is: What does it mean to serve?

When you serve, you are doing something for another person. At the heart of service is putting the interests of others above your own. The only way to have a heart of service is by actually caring for others.

As I told the audience, you don't have to join the military to serve. You can serve others in your school, family, work, church, and community in many ways. But, you have to care first.

However, the desire to serve appears to be lukewarm at best. Much like the small percentage of Americans who have served in the military, there seems to be only a small percentage of businesses that understand what it means to serve employees and customers. We see it daily in our interactions at the post office, the grocery store, restaurants or while trying to get help online or on the phone. Indifference and obstacles seem to be more prevalent than attention and a clear path. Good customer service and engaged employees just seem to be the exception rather than the rule these days.

But it doesn't have to be this way.

There are some great companies with leaders who understand how a service-focused culture helps increase sales and profitability as well as improve customer and employee retention. These leaders realize that service helps their organizations stand out and succeed. These are leaders who care.

And you should care, too.

This need for a return to service is why this book is so important. Neal Woodson understands the importance of service. He knows that service is the business of business. As I say in my books, leadership is a people business. Leaders who build a service-focused culture help employees and customers succeed. They create the places where people want to work and where they enjoy doing business.

What you will read in this book is not taught in business schools. Service is the secret sauce that allows ordinary organizations to become extraordinary.

I hope you enjoy this book as much as I did and that you become one of the small percentage of business leaders who give a $#!+.

Jon S. Rennie, bestselling author of *I Have the Watch: Becoming a Leader Worth Following*

Introduction

"It is easy to hate and it is difficult to love. This is how the whole scheme of things works. All good things are difficult to achieve; and bad things are very easy to get."
-Confucius

Have you ever had to return an item to a store and you made up a story so the store would more readily take the item back? Maybe you got home and, upon further analysis, realized that you really didn't like the item as much as you first thought, or you overspent in a fit of shopping passion and can't really afford it after all. But you know the store will balk at that "real" reason so you make up something like, "it didn't fit" or "it didn't look right in the room" or some such thing. Then, you use the little white lie …ahem…story… to try and make things easier.

But why these games? Why do we, the customers, have to do such things to get around obstacles? Why are there obstacles at all? Why does it look as if business is regularly cooking up ways to make it easier and less costly for them while making it more difficult for customers? Why does it seem like things are purposely done to get in the way so customers will get out of the way? I know in my experience, being a customer these days is anything but a walk in the park. In fact, it would appear customer life is, in many cases, as much work as work life.

Think about it. How many times have you heard friends, family, or coworkers talk about their woes as customers? Whether it's having to find a receipt, get into contact with a manager, make innumerable calls, or any number of other inconvenient things, "nothing is ever easy" seems to be a common refrain.

It makes no sense. There was a day when businesses wanted to be helpful. There was a day when businesses took pride in obliging people. There was a day when businesses would jump through hoops to make sure customers were taken care of.

Why does it seem those days have left us? Is it me? Am I just being too negative or overly pessimistic?

I don't think so. The statistics appear to support what I am seeing. Here are just a few.

- 80% of people regularly have negative experiences with customer service. (Freshworks)
- 70% of customers have stopped doing business with a brand due to a poor customer service experience. (Verint)
- Only 20% of service issues are resolved in most businesses. (McKinsey)

- 53% of customers believe companies don't take any action on customer feedback. (Zippia)

Businesses are making a big mistake. They are missing a big part of the game. While consistently delivering the product you said you would deliver is a worthy goal, it's only half the work.

Doing business has two major components: 1) delivery (getting the job done), and 2) interaction (relating and collaborating with people). Most businesses focus primarily on delivery while only an enlightened few place as much emphasis on interaction. This is mostly because the delivery portion is easy to measure and correlate to the bottom line. However, since humans base a large part of their decisions on how they feel, being an unenlightened believer in the what-gets-measured-is-all-that-matters game can be a mistake.

All of this brings up a couple of questions, 1) why have things come to this, and 2) what can be done about it?

In this book, we are going to go on a journey to answer these questions. We will begin by looking at a fundamental missing link in the evolution of business that stands beneath the larger issues. Then, with two brief stories—one about how an organization can get things wrong, and another about how a few compassionate souls can get it so right— we will see the powerful influence of this fundamental link and how, sadly, the second story is, more times than not, out of the norm. From there, we will get a better understanding as to why this is with a history lesson that looks at how our collective consciousness has been misled about human nature and how the fallout from that has impacted business and done so much damage. Finally, we will peek at an organization and an individual who intuitively found a formula that overcomes these obstacles and allows any organization and any individual contributor to begin making changes for the better.

Along the way, I will riff, rant, tell stories, and share tips coming from years of observing the world of work and teaching ways to improve it.

Now, while I wrote this book to help create positive change in our businesses and our lives, I also wrote it to start conversations. Conversations are what spark ideas and ideas change things. And we need change, change for the better. We need better workplaces and better buying spaces because we're all workers and buyers and making those things better would make life better for everyone. So, when you finish the book, share it, share ideas, start conversations, and make change.

Okay?

Let's roll on.

PART ONE: SETTING THE STAGE

Chapter 1

The Magic Bullet

"At the center of your being you have the answer."
-Lao Tzu

On one particularly pleasant Saturday morning, as I was playing golf with some friends, the typical banter about family and sports turned to work. Knowing that I was a teacher and coach of leadership development and service improvement, a member of our foursome who owns his own business asked me what he should tell his employees so they would deliver great service.

My mind began racing through multiple possibilities. I wanted to give him something meaningful yet practical. In what seemed like a long period of thought—it was actually less than a minute—I looked up and said, "You have to give a $#!+." He looked a little stunned. I think he thought I would have said something much more eloquent and complicated, but instead, as is often my want, I opted for edgy and to the point. Then, after a minute or so of digesting things, he looked at me and asked, "Is that it?"

"Yeah, pretty much," I said, "but it's not just about them giving a $#!+, you must give a $#!+ as well. In fact, everyone in your organization from you to your administrative staff to your managers to, yes, your frontline, customer-facing team members must give a $#!+. And they have to give a $#!+ not only about the work they do and getting the job done, but about the wellbeing of the people they do it for. If giving a $#!+ about others, employees and customers alike, is not part of your entire culture, it will all be for naught, and the organization will never see the true benefit."

With that, we moved on to other topics and carried on playing.

Now, while nothing in my "you have to give a $#!+" comment seems too earth shattering, it was a sort of enlightenment for me because it sparked a flame to go on a journey to find more meaning in those words.

I initially thought giving a $#!+ was about caring, which, according to dictionaries, is typically defined as the act of being concerned (a.k.a. troubled by or worried) about something, someone, or both.

But was that really it? I wasn't satisfied. So, after tripping over a Twitter post about compassion, I began to research that.

I had never really considered compassion as part of the discussion here, in fact, I had never really reflected on what it was at all. I had always equated compassion with church, charities, love, etc. It didn't seem at all something that would fit with anything to do with business. But I was wrong. Very wrong.

Compassion is defined as an emotional response to another's pain or suffering involving an authentic desire to help. Thus, compassion is comprised of two parts, awareness and action. And while it is related to empathy, it is the emphasis on action that largely differentiates it.

As I looked at and pondered the definition, it struck me that compassion has a not-too-distant relationship to business. In fact, in so many ways, it is precisely what business is about.

Being aware of the needs, wants, and yes, even the suffering of people followed by a desire to help them solve their problems, that is business in a nutshell.

And yes, I know there is a transaction involved, but in its essence, it would appear that business is or should be a compassionate enterprise.

And while this insight was enlightening on its own, I still had a nagging feeling that there was something more. As I continued researching, I found a TED Talk on compassion by Daniel Goleman, one of the foremost authorities on Emotional Intelligence.

In the TED Talk, Goleman tells a story about being in the subway in New York City where he saw a man lying at the bottom of the stairs leading to the platform. The man was slumped on the ground and not moving. People were thoughtlessly stepping over him to get where they were going. It was as if he were a minor obstacle and not a human being. Goleman, though, decided to do something. He reached out and helped the man sit up. As it turned out, the man had passed out due to hunger. He was homeless and hadn't eaten in days. Goleman spoke with him, and as he spoke, others took interest.

One person went and got the man a hot dog, another gave him a sandwich and a cup of coffee, and a subway police officer gave him a blanket.

What Goleman realized was that he made a big impact by simply noticing. And that simple act of noticing led to helping the man, which is, by definition, compassion.

But that raised a question, why did Goleman notice? What caused him to be the one who didn't step over the man? What caused him to go out of his way to help?

As I pondered this, I was reminded of a time I had gone out of my way years before while working in a hotel's convention and meeting space.

I was in my office when one of my team members peeked their head in the door and said, "She's crying."

"Who's crying?" I said.

"There's a woman on stage in the ballroom crying."

I immediately made my way to find out what the problem was. I was deliberate in my approach as I did not want to startle her. I carefully went up the couple of steps and gently asked, "Excuse me ma'am, are you hurt? Have you fallen?"

Trying to pull herself together, sniffing and snorting, she said, "No, I forgot my prop."

The group she was with was running fashion shows to show off the different lines of clothing that they had created for the next season. In her role, she oversaw infant fashions.

"Okay, what's your prop?" I asked.

"A baby doll, I have to have a baby doll to show off the clothes. I'm going to lose my job. I can't do this fashion show without a baby doll."

My mind began racing. I thought to myself, *my daughter is 5 years old and I've got a house full of baby dolls*. I looked at the woman and told her that if she would give me 20 minutes, I could help her.

I left the hotel, drove to my house, went into my daughter's room, found a baby doll that was decent— meaning clean, with arms, legs, and hair intact—and drove back to the hotel. When I arrived, I made a beeline into the ballroom and handed my daughter's beloved baby doll to the shaken infant-fashion director. Now the real waterworks began, she cried and gave me a big hug. But this time they were tears of joy. Hell, I almost cried myself. I was so happy that I had made her happy.

But why did I do it? Was it so I could feel good? Well, that didn't cross my mind at the time. Was it to show off? No. Again, not something rolling around in my head. Was it my job? No, I didn't have to do it. I could have told my teammate to deal with it. I could have found excuses for not being able to do anything. But I didn't. Why? Was it because I am a saintly person? Hardly. So what was it?

What I realized was that when I heard about a woman crying, I stopped thinking of myself. I lost all concern for my own needs and had a willingness to go out of my way. I was willing to be inconvenienced.

And there it was. There was the thing Goleman and I had in common. That was what came before any compassionate act. We both had more than concern, we had a willingness to be inconvenienced. We were willing to stop. We were both willing to do that which all those who stepped over the man on the platform did not. We were willing to take time to get out of our own skin and see what was going on.

And with that, I had found the real meaning behind my "give a $#!+" pronouncement on the golf course. It's about willingness. Willingness to sacrifice and be inconvenienced. Willingness to give up time and personal pursuits to see others. Ultimately, it is what makes compassion possible. It is what makes us pause to notice the hungry man on the subway platform or to go out of our way to make someone happy.

Without it, all the concern in the world is pointless. Without it, we are just like those who stepped over the hungry man on the subway platform. Without it, we don't pause to notice.

So now, when someone asks me for the magic bullet for great service, this is it, "You must give a $#!+. You must be willing to be inconvenienced. And, you must do it before anything else if you want to truly up your game to deliver help that changes things and makes lives better."

Sounds simple, and in many ways it is, but there are things standing in the way, and largely, they come from how we have been hoodwinked, deceived, and duped. For centuries, we have been taught a story that gives a rather bleak account of human nature. And it is this story that has come down to us and influenced so much of what we do on a day-to-day basis.

I want to look at this story and the issues it has created and then plant seeds for a new story. A new story that enables better choices. But I am not a psychologist or a behavioral scientist so I am not going to present a tome discussing how to turn your life around or improve all your personal relationships. Rather, I am going to take a different track. I am going to look at the business world and how, by bringing a new narrative and new tactics, we can do better work and build a better world.

We will begin by looking at what it's like when our magic bullet is missing and then what it's like when it's there.

Chapter 2

When It's Missing and When It's Not

"Beware of missing chances; otherwise it may be altogether too late some day."
–Franz Liszt

When It's Missing

My wife was out of town on business and her birthday was coming up so I wanted to send her flowers.

Before calling a florist, I wanted to make sure things would go smoothly so I called the front desk of my wife's hotel first. "Hi, I'm going to have some flowers delivered. Can I have them brought to the front desk? I want to make sure they get to her room promptly and are placed on the table in the room so she sees them immediately when she walks in at the end of the day." Their reply? "We'd be happy to take care of that for you."

With my master plan coming together, I rang one of the big national internet florists and told them about my wife being out of town and how I needed the flowers taken to the front desk so they could be placed in her room. My thought was that since I set this up with the hotel, I had made it easy.

This is when I heard the words, "I'm sorry, but we can't do that. We can only deliver to wherever the hotel takes deliveries and that is usually the loading dock." Now floating in my head were images of the loading dock with smelly dumpsters and grimy floors. I could just see the flowers laying on the dock and someone walking on them having not seen them or throwing them away thinking they were trash. I protested. "What do you mean? I'm not asking for anything crazy, just drop them at the front desk. C'mon, I spoke with the hotel and they said it was fine."

"I'm sorry sir, this is our policy, and we can only drop them where deliveries are taken." Ugh, there it was, policy, the dreaded word and dodge for every employee who is just doing their job. I did a little more protesting but was met with more "policy" and "we can't do it" so I gave up. I told her that I thought their policy was ridiculous and that I would find someone else who was more flexible.

Needless to say, I was stunned by the florist's response. I couldn't believe it. I wasn't asking them to climb a mountain or anything. I just wanted them to honor a simple, easy request. But no. The policy was the policy.

When It's Present

Once, when my children were very young, my wife took them to Scotland to visit her parents, and after a lovely time with grandma and grandpa, it came time to fly back home. The journey began in Edinburgh and included a stop at London Heathrow to change planes for the long leg back to North America.

Upon arrival at Heathrow, a problem came up. The passengers heading for the USA were informed that there was an issue with the plane they were to be boarding for the Atlantic crossing, and, due to this, they would have to stay overnight at a hotel near the airport until a replacement aircraft could be found and readied for the completion of the trip.

This sent my wife into a bit of a panic. You see, she had only brought enough diapers for the original journey. She had nothing for any extension. She was now going to be stuck with both kids in a hotel room with nothing to do and no diapers.

Fortunately, one of the flight attendants noticed my wife's discomfort. She asked her what was wrong and, after hearing all about it, jumped into action. She spoke with the rest of the flight attendants and then told my wife they had a plan and to stay on the plane until she returned.

After most of the passengers deplaned, the flight attendant came back to my wife. She helped gather up personal belongings and led her and the kids to an awaiting van conveniently parked by the plane. They were then whisked away to the hotel adjacent to the airport where the driver helped with bags and got my wife and kids checked in and safely deposited in the room.

After a few moments getting settled, a knock came at the door, and when my wife opened it, who was there but the flight attendants with bags full of diapers, coloring books, and toys to make for a more pleasant evening. They also let my wife know that they had taken care of meals as well. Instead of having to bother with going to the hotel restaurant, all my wife had to do was order room service for dinner and breakfast in the morning. Additionally, they had also taken care of getting her back to the airport for the flight the next day.

After a pleasant dinner in the room and a decent night's sleep, my wife got the kids up and ready and had the room-service breakfast. Then, a knock came at the door where a van driver stood ready to escort them back to the airport, get them through security, and onto the awaiting plane.

The result? My wife got home, told me the story, and was ecstatic about the entire experience. She even wrote a long letter to the CEO of the airline cheering the flight attendants and the incredible service.

Contrast

Two very different stories. One of how an organization got it wrong. How it appeared they didn't give a $#!+. Not the young lady on the call mind you, she was just following orders, no, the organization didn't give a $#!+. They were unwilling to be inconvenienced by seeing things from the customer's point of view. They were unwilling to be inconvenienced to consider doing things differently. They were unwilling to be inconvenienced to think beyond their needs first.

The second story, however, showed how it can be different. It showed what it was to give a $#!+. It showed how a willingness to be inconvenienced by compassion can create magical moments, and how a willingness to be inconvenienced to improve the lives of others can make a difference.

Sadly though, given the current state of the service we typically receive, story two is, by and large, an anomaly. Why is this so, why is it the exception rather than the rule? And, is it possible to make it more of the rule? Well, yes, I believe it is possible to make it more of the rule, but before we look at that, let's first get some answers as to why this lack of giving a $#!+ has become so widespread.

Chapter 3

A History Lesson

"To kill an error is as good a service as, and sometimes even better than, the establishing of a new truth or fact."
-Charles Darwin

Service. It's not fancy. It's not complicated. It's just helping people. That's it. Look it up. "The action of helping someone."

If you do an internet search, you get a series of definitions and then a smattering of things like the

National Weather Service, the Internal Revenue Service, and businesses who have service in their names. But almost nowhere do you see anything about how vital service is and has been to our human history and our very survival. And why? Because it's for the weak and our nature proves it.

It's Weak

When you mention service, for many people, their first thought is customer service. However, service—helping people—is so much more than a job or role in a business. Service is something that is quintessentially human. While we are not the only animals to be helpful, we are one of the few who will do things to benefit others without the need for reciprocation.

Additionally, serving others by being helpful and cooperative—commonly known as prosocial behavior—is something we all do almost from the moment we wake up in the morning to the time we drift off to sleep. If you make coffee for your spouse, partner, or roommate in the morning, service. If you help get the kids ready for school, service. If you help a colleague with a report, service. If you pick up milk on the way home, service. We do it as an almost automatic part of our lives. We help family, friends, and coworkers constantly. In fact, it would seem helping others is something we almost can't stop doing.

Yet, we still undervalue its importance. We, for eons, have placed people who are in service roles beneath us. Think of the millions of people exploited, enslaved, and forced to serve. Think of servants who, even though paid for their work and not in the clutches of slavery, were seen as lower class and expected to unquestioningly do the bidding of their employer.

Today, we see all kinds of holdovers of these sensibilities. It's not uncommon to hear derisive language being used to describe "service roles."

Phrases like "they'll get a 'real' job soon" are all too common when people hear of someone working in a restaurant or retail.

You see, we like service when we are being served, but we hate the thought being expected to do it. And given history's legacy, it makes sense. However, this is a narrow view. This sees service only in the light of being *in service of* someone, i.e., being controlled, and dismisses the noble notion that being *of service to* someone can be and is so much more. Being "of service to" in contrast to being "in service of" is about bringing value. And bringing value to others to help them accomplish things, well, what could be more respectable and worthy of our admiration? Yet, the stigma goes on and service is derided and mocked.

It's Not Our Nature

We've been hoodwinked, duped, and led down a garden path.

Humans, in one form or another, have been on this planet for about 300,000 years, and for the majority of it, we have been cooperative. We have built great cities, conquered diseases, designed engineering marvels, and traveled to the stars, not because we grinded away in solitary genius, but because we worked together. Service, it would seem, is our human superpower, and we've been demonstrating it since we first appeared on the planet.

We began life as hunter-gatherers stalking beasts and foraging for plants. And, much to the chagrin of those who would like us to believe we were violent, competitive, selfish savages, we worked together to do it. We had to.

We are not and never have been the biggest, fastest, or strongest in the animal kingdom. So, as hunters, we had to go as a group in order to get dinner and not be dinner.

As gatherers, going together just made sense. One person searching can never match many people searching. If you misplace your keys, do you search alone, or do you call out for help? When the kids and the spouse or partner fan out, the keys get found. So it goes with foraging for food.

Scientists have confirmed all of this in studies on existing hunter-gatherer groups. These groups work together. They prize cooperation and helpfulness while punishing competition and selfishness. They get it. To thrive, we must serve.

Our prehistoric cousins got it too. Cooperating, working together, and helping each other is how to survive.

But that got lost. About 10,000 to 12,000 years ago, things began to change. We started learning how to farm and raise livestock. As hunter-gathers, it was all about *we* surviving, but as farmers, it started to be more about *me* surviving. As we did our own work and cultivated our own food, it became ours, a possession. Thus, we chose to, or maybe felt we had to, defend it. Here began the journey down the road to what we believe about our nature today.

But it has not been a straight path; there have been turns on the road. In a hearkening back to our cooperative beginnings, someone got the idea to trade. "If I have pigs and you have chickens, why not share with each other and we can have variety?" Thus, life was no longer just about surviving, it was about thriving as well.

Then, in another turn, someone came along and realized that they could trade things for labor. Perhaps giving someone a pig for cleaning the hut for example. What this did was to equate having more with doing less, and thus, living an easier life. Now, life was about more than surviving and thriving, it was about winning. It was about having more because more meant power. More meant you could do what you wanted with anyone you wanted whenever you wanted. Thus began the win-to-get-more game, and it's the game we've been playing for the last several thousand years. We've gone from surviving to surviving-and-thriving to surviving-and-thriving-by-winning.

And to perpetuate this surviving-and-thriving-by-winning game, we've told stories, stories that say selfish competition is our nature and how we succeed. From biblical tales to Thomas Hobbes to the ramblings of Ayn Rand, we've been told that humans are self-interested fighters and any goodness is just a facade. Richard Dawkins even goes as far as telling us that our genes are selfish.

A great example of this storytelling comes in one of the most lauded books of the 20th century, William Golding's Lord of the Flies. In its pages, we are told a tale that supports what we've been led to believe. After a plane crash, several boys get stranded on a deserted island and slowly resort to savagery, their "true" nature. When they are rescued, three youngsters have been murdered and the island reduced to a wasteland. And are we surprised? No. This is what we have accepted as who we are at our core. Competing for everything is what we must do to have a successful life.

And while the evils around us and the self-interest that abounds suggest that this story of our human vice is true, we see inklings that tell a different story. We see inklings that tell us that we are more. We are nobler. We do have angels of a better nature.

In 1965, near Tonga, in a real-life Lord of the Flies, six boys trying to escape a boarding school they hated, stole a boat and set sail for a better place. A storm damaged the boat and they got stranded on a deserted island. But they didn't resort to competitive power struggles, they resorted to cooperation. They did not become savages. They worked together and created a civilized community. When they were rescued, there were no murders and no wasteland. Yet, this is not the story we study. This is not the story we are taught. This is not the human nature we have come to accept. Thus, stories like the Tongan schoolboys are usually tossed off as one-off coincidences.

But what about other examples of our better angels, are they just coincidences too? Infants, without prompting or training, reach out to help others pick up dropped items, toddlers open doors for people whose hands are full, teenagers start charity campaigns, adults come out in numbers to offer aid when disaster strikes, first responders run into danger to save strangers, and the list goes on. That's a lot of coincidences.

And what about the "coincidence" of Mother Nature? She too seems to be telling a counter story to win-at-all-costs.

In the mid-1990s, a group of researchers did a study on prosocial behaviors like cooperation, helpfulness, generosity, and kindness in college students. What they found was that those who were more prosocial were seen as more attractive for dating than those who were not prosocial. What this suggests is that Mother Nature has made helpfulness better insurance against loneliness and, perhaps, even a good bet for having a successful sex life. And if those assertions sound a bit of a stretch to you, at minimum, I think you have to agree that Mother Nature has made prosocial behavior an advantage rather than a weakness.

Furthermore, this social, sexual incenting is not all. Mother Nature also provides a chemical push for cooperative helpfulness in the form of the hormone oxytocin. This chemical, often called the love hormone, is responsible for creating bonds and connection. It stimulates two neurotransmitters, dopamine and serotonin, that give us a positive, warm feeling of confidence and optimism, and is released when we cuddle with our mothers in childhood, during intimacy, and when we help and give to others.

And it's not only provided to givers; it is doled out to receivers, and, to make it even more impactful, onlookers as well. Those who give, receive, or merely see or hear about kindness and helpfulness, all get a hit of this feel-good cocktail. And when people feel good, they want to feel good again. So…they help again. And because it's not limited to givers and receivers, the circle of helpfulness widens. And as the circle widens, a community of helpful cooperation begins to build. And a helpful, cooperative community is a community much more likely to survive and thrive.

And speaking of thriving, oxytocin has another distinct benefit. It suppresses cortisol, the stress hormone. And by doing that, we get health benefits like lower blood pressure, less heart disease, faster healing, less chronic pain, better mental health, and longer life.

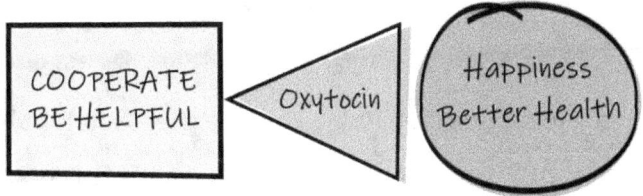

Given all of this, it appears Mother Nature would prefer we cooperate and help each other. She knows our survival is much more likely in peaceful cooperation than in warring competition.

Nevertheless, the drumbeat of the selfish-competition story goes on. "It's a dog-eat-dog world so do whatever you must to win" is what we hear and see on a regular basis. So, that's what's embedded in our collective consciousness. That's how we proceed. We selfishly compete. It has become who we are despite the contradiction with our inner helper.

And with the speed of communication afforded to us with the internet, the message that we are competitive and selfish at our core is propagated in ways both subtle and overt to hundreds of millions of people 24 hours a day, every day. Thus, our better angels get stifled, and easy excuses get made for all kinds of repellent behavior. It has created a metaphorical train wreck in the business world for both employees and customers.

So, like rubberneckers on the highway, let's take a look at the train wreck.

Chapter 4

The Business of Business

"I think that there is nothing, not even crime, more opposed to poetry, to philosophy, ay, to life itself than this incessant business."
–Henry David Thoreau

My father worked for a major railroad. And in one part of his career, he was responsible for managing the cleanup of train wrecks.

I once went to one of the wreck sites with him, and it was a mess. Huge train cars had been tossed around like toys. Cargo was strewn about for miles. All manner of liquids were leaking everywhere. It was terrible. I could only imagine the impact on the people living nearby and how the environment would suffer over the longer term. The lesson? Getting off track has many consequences.

Now consider the story about the self-focused florist. Like a speeding train with an engineer not paying attention to the track ahead, they got derailed. They got off track and lost sight of what business is all about, which, regrettably, happens far more frequently than not.

But why is this the case? What exactly is behind this derailment? Let's take a closer look.

I was at a conference getting some coffee at a break table where a fellow attendee and I picked up a conversation.

"What do you do?" he asked.

"I coach and teach leadership and service improvement mostly in the hospitality space," I said.

"So, you're in the service business," my new friend replied.

"So are you," I quickly remarked.

Looking both annoyed and puzzled, he countered, "No, I'm in the financial business."

With this, I went a little deeper to clarify my position.

"Do you help people plan for retirement?"

"Yes."

"Do you help people save for their kids' education?"

"Yes."

"Do you help people create a strategy for buying a home?"

"Yes."

"So you help people."

"Yes."

"You're in the service business."

You see, every business is in the service business. Every single one.

Every business does one, two, or all three of the following. They help people...

- Do things they don't want to do.
- Do things they don't know how to do.
- Access things they can't readily access.

If I want a shirt, I don't know how to sew one, and, quite frankly, don't want to know how to sew one, so I go to a clothing store where they help me.

If I have a leaky pipe in my house, I don't know how to fix it, so I call a plumber to help me solve the problem.

Think of any business, they all help people by creating and delivering value, and that is service. Service is their primary purpose. Service is the business of business.

And if you are thinking this is far-fetched, pie-in-the-sky, unicorns-and-rainbows thinking, consider these thoughts from some leading thinkers in the world of business and management.

"To satisfy the customer is the mission and purpose of every business."
-Peter Drucker, management consultant, educator, and author

"The sole purpose of business is service."
-Leo Burnett, pioneering advertising executive

"Every business is a service business."
-Philip Kotler, author, marketing consultant, and professor emeritus, Kellogg School of Management at Northwestern University

"There is no other business than a service business."
-Robert Lusch, business professor, University of Arizona Business School, co-creator of the Service-Dominant Logic framework

"Organizations are established to serve human needs. There is no other reason for their existence."
–Stephen R. Covey, educator, author, businessman, and speaker

"Organizations exist to serve. Period."

–Tom Peters, author, management expert, humanist

And there are some companies that have realized it, too. I did some work awhile back for an audio-visual production company called Projection. To learn more about them before our first meeting, I looked at their mission, vision, and core values. The first of their core values was labeled Client First, and the little blurb to describe it said, "Our mission is to help [customers] achieve theirs." My first thought was "hurray, here is a company that gets it. This should be the mission of every business." But then it occurred to me, "it *is* the mission of every business."

But there's a big problem. Most businesses and business people, like my daunted coffee-break companion, have lost touch with this. They do not see that the true purpose of business is service. They either don't know it or don't see it as important.

Put simply, business doesn't know what business it's in. This is where things have derailed. And like William Golding's Lord-of-the-Flies boys who lost sight of their values and lacked a sense of virtuous purpose, there's a lot of negative fallout.

Let's look at three particularly damaging consequences.

- Profit-first mentality
- People management
- Sidelining of human concerns

"Don't think money does everything or you are going to end up doing everything for money."
-Voltaire

Profit-first mentality

Take a breath.

Take another.

Now, do that for an hour and write down how many breaths you take. I will wait.

…

…

…

Did you do it?

No? Why not?

Look, breathing is the purpose of life, this is important.

Let's try again. Count your breaths for an hour. Then, count them for two hours. Then, for 8 hours.

How many breaths are you taking per hour? This is important. Do you have a number? Because what I want you to do now is create a strategy for taking more breaths each day.

If you are now scratching your head wondering what the hell I'm getting at, good, because what I'm getting at is this. Every day in our businesses, we do this same thing, we just do it with money.

Is breathing the purpose of life? Of course not—at least I hope you see the purpose of your life as more than breathing. Even people like severe asthmatics who have critical breathing challenges don't think breathing is the point in life. Do they focus on it at certain times? Yes. But is it the point of their existence? No.

However, we must all recognize that breathing is necessary to live, it's just not the reason we live. And that's the crux of the matter. We live for more. We live to make a difference. We live to keep the species going and hopefully leave the planet better when we depart than it was when we came in.

Yet, the logic here disappears when we talk about business. Why do we make profit our priority rather than the real reason business exists? Why has service, the reason we do the work, get marginalized? How have we lost our way?

To answer that, we'll need another history lesson.

In 1776, the Scottish economist Adam Smith published a book called the Wealth of Nations that formulated ideas that would become the foundation for what we now know as capitalism.

Largely, the ideas presented centered on something he called the 'invisible hand' of commerce. This metaphor was used to describe the way society and the economy could benefit from the accrued, self-interested actions of people. But Smith was specific, he did not say just any people, he specifically called them virtuous individuals.

Why that term? What did he mean by virtuous?

Well, before writing the Wealth of Nations, Smith wrote another book called the Theory of Moral Sentiments. In it he planted the seed for the Wealth of Nations by providing the philosophical guardrails necessary for the invisible-hand concept to be moral. And one of the key guardrails was this idea of the virtuous individual, who is defined as someone who is mindful of taking actions in their own self-interest while at the same time considering the impact of those actions on the interests of a larger whole. This consideration of others is what creates the uplifting, enlightened invisible hand of commerce that regulates itself morally.

What gets missed in our modern version of Smith's ideas is the piece about not being solely self-interested but also being mindful of the impact of those interests on others. Today's capitalism is not Smith's capitalism. And while this shift from Smith's enlightened, virtuous self-interest to something quite a bit more tarnished was an increasing problem throughout history, it had not fully imprinted on our collective consciousness until someone opened Pandora's Box.

That took place in 1970 with the publication of a New York Times article authored by Nobel Prize-winning economist Milton Friedman. In this article, Friedman pronounced that "there is one and only one social responsibility of business—to use its resources to engage in activities designed to increase its profits." And although the article had a lot of details surrounding that pronouncement, business leaders the world over began latching onto its headline theme as a license to go out and spare nothing in making as much money as possible.

"In one fell swoop," in the words of the late Lynn Stout, Professor of Corporate & Business Law at Cornell Law School, "Milton Friedman persuaded a generation that selfishness was the natural state of humanity, and that selfishness ultimately would lead to the best possible society."

And while this greed-is-good thinking has fueled economies and made some people very wealthy, overall, the outcomes have not been so good.

- Exorbitant pay at the top levels creating a huge gap between "haves" and "have nots."
- Shady accounting practices and a craze for share buy-backs that skew stock prices and business valuations.
- Financial resources being diverted from needed investments in innovation.

- Manufacturing jobs steadily sent to countries with cheaper labor costs making public corporations job destroyers instead of job creators.

- Almost all gains flowing from improvements in productivity being allocated to shareholders instead of workers.

- Deployment of more top-down command-and-control management to drive productivity because making money for shareholders and top executives doesn't inspire it.

- Workplace policies and non-compete agreements that prohibit over 30 million workers in the U.S. from leaving their job to work for a competitor or to start a competing business.

- The use of layoffs as tools for creating beefier bottom lines that benefit shareholders/investors/top execs at the expense of working people and families.

And if those ill consequences aren't enough to see that profit-first thinking is flawed, let's consider the logic problem.

We will start with an indisputable fact. Without customers there is no money…and no business.

This leads directly to the logic problem: profit cannot come first because, without customers, there is no profit. Customers must come first.

This is not like the chicken or egg puzzle where an argument can be made for either preceding the other. The relationship between customers and profit is a one-way street. One (profit) comes only out of the other (customers) and it cannot be the other way around. You simply cannot have profit with customers coming second. It just cannot be. You must provide something that customers find valuable enough to pay for and then manage your operation in a way where you are left with profit. If you want more profit, you must innovate to provide more value and then manage well, that is it, and it all starts with customers.

If you have ever been to a ball game of any sort and watched a player drop a catch because, instead of watching the ball into their hands, they looked away thinking of what they would do after the catch, you know what I mean. You must do the right things first to get a good outcome. You must concentrate on catching (service) first if you want to make the great run (profit).

But don't think I am dismissing the need for profit, I am not. Businesses need profit, but by over-emphasizing it they are missing the opportunity service brings in maximizing it. Let's look at a simple example.

If we agree that service is helping people, it follows that one of the outcomes of that helping is to make things easier for someone. For example, if I need help moving a large table in my house and you give me a hand, I expend less effort than if I were to try and do it myself. Thus, to serve is largely to remove effort.

With this in mind, I want you to imagine your morning cup of coffee and consider the different ways you can get it.

One way is to go to the grocery store and buy a bag of coffee beans. You bring it home. You grind the beans, boil water, measure the right amount for your cup, brew it, fill your mug, and add cream, sugar, or whatever else you like to make it your special elixir. For that, you pay anywhere from 30¢ to 50¢ a cup. But who does all the work? You do.

A second way to get your coffee is to go to a convenience store. When you go this route, the coffee has been ground, measured, brewed, etc. and all you need to do is fill your cup, add cream, and you are on your way. Cost? About $1.50. Work? Both you and the provider, the store, had to do things.

The third way to get that morning brew, is to go to a coffee shop. There, you walk in, place an order, wait a few minutes, and there it is. They do everything. Then, you go and sit in a nice comfortable chair, listen to music, and use their WiFi. Cost? About $3.50. Effort? Almost zero. And, there's the added bonus of some additional comfort.

The following is a visual model of this concept.

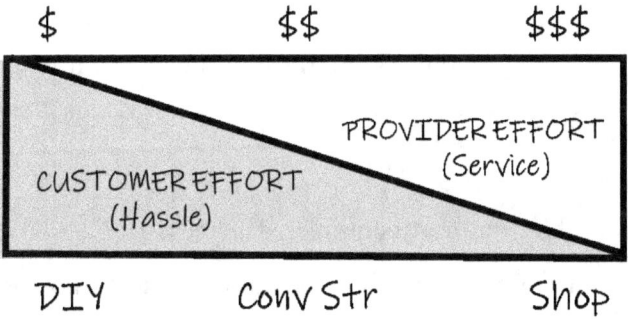

By taking away customer effort—effectively providing *more* service, and in the case of the coffee shop, *better* service—you deliver more value for which customers will pay a premium.

And there are examples in many places. Think about the difference between budget, minimum-service, full-service, and luxury hotels. With each step up the ladder, you get more service—more effort removed—and a higher price tag.

The same is true with fast-service, full-service, and five-star restaurants. With each step, better food, more help, more ambience, more personal treatment, and more revenue for the business.

Service is not only the purpose of business, it is the way to greater success.

Yet, the drumbeat continues. Business leaders have bought into the belief that breathing is the purpose of life and thus is trying to amass as much air as possible. As Lynn Stout put it, it is selfishness, and it runs completely afoul of and in opposition to the true reason for business, not to mention being illogical.

"Speak softly and carry a big stick."
-Theodore Roosevelt

People Management

I was talking to a friend the other day who had just come from a meeting with their boss. They had been reprimanded for not asking for permission to do something.

Yet, what they did was done with the best of intentions, did no harm, and came at a nominal cost. They only did it to make the organization better. They did it to make sure customers saw the organization in the right light.

When they replied to their boss with their reasoning, their boss told them that though the intentions were good, they still needed to get permission. However, they did not want this to stifle their creativity and initiative. To this my friend replied, "But you just did."

Frederick Winslow Taylor's early 1900's thinking on management strategy where the decision-making thinkers are separated from the laboring doers has been the default arrangement for over one hundred years. It's a very productive scheme because it enables the maximum amount of work to get done. Since the doers are not distracted by the complications of time-consuming decision making, they can spend all of their time getting the job done leaving a hierarchy of thinkers (management) to ensure, through command and control, that numbers, quotas, and production levels stay high.

Taylor's thinking was based around his Scientific Management system which was created for achieving efficient execution of known, repeatable processes at scale. Essentially, this management strategy was the product of an environment where factories with assembly lines ruled the day.

Are you familiar with the I Love Lucy show? It was on air from 1951 to 1957 and starred Lucille Ball as

Lucy Ricardo. Her best friend was Ethel Mertz played by Vivian Vance.

In one hilarious episode, Lucy and Ethel go to work in a chocolate factory. Their jobs are to pick up chocolate pieces moving on a conveyor belt, place them neatly in wrappers, and put them back on the belt to be boxed up down the line.

It all begins sedately enough and the ladies keep up nicely. Each chocolate gets wrapped cleanly. However, this soon changes when the manager comes in and, looking for more production, ratchets up the speed of the conveyor belt. The chocolates start coming fast and furious. The girls cannot keep up so they start eating missed pieces. They put them down their blouses. They toss them in their hats. They do anything to hide their mistakes. And while this scene might be hilarious, it is a great example of the problems with Taylorist management.

In Taylor's Industrial Age vision, people are to be run like machines with strict commands to control their every move. Essentially, they are to be seen as tools that do one thing, do it well, and do it all day. The goal is to get the most out of people in order to get more results in the shortest amount of time. Management is about control, and it is the approach we have subscribed to for over 100 years.

The problem is that when the goal is to get the most out of people rather than the best out of people, the Lucys and Ethels of the world get frustrated by the monotony and driven mad by the mindlessness. They get stressed by the constant push, and fear losing their jobs when they make a mistake or can't keep up. So, they begin cutting corners, hiding, faking, or cheating.

And what happens? The committed people—those who can think and do great work—move on, leaving the organization with compliant people—those who keep their thinking to themselves and do "good enough" work—and indifferent people—those who don't think and only do the bare minimum. Organizations must then cope with a workforce whose best is mediocrity.

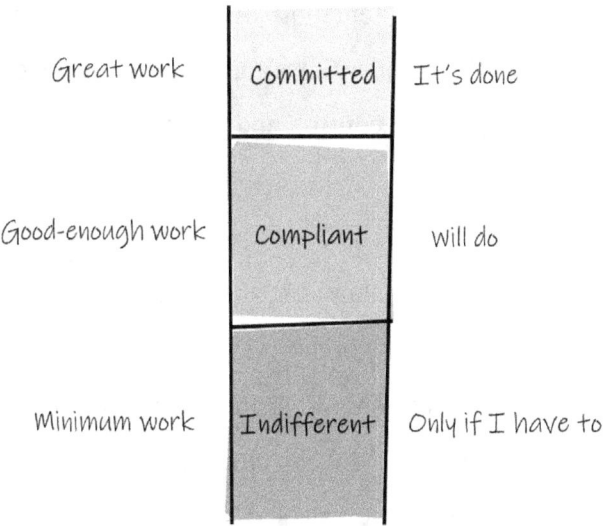

However, even with all of its limitations and challenges, management of people through command and control has been the standard practice for most organizations. Produce, produce, produce has been the clarion call.

Nowhere did this need to manage (a.k.a., control) people make itself more apparent than during the pandemic of 2020-21. As people were being forced into working from home due to lockdown, managers everywhere were in mortal fear that employees would run amok reneging on their work duties. Consequently, many articles appeared with advice on how to keep order, control, and production high. For example…

- Employees should let managers know when they take any breaks.
- Employees should share calendars to ensure mangers know when employees are available and where they are at all times.
- Employees should answer all calls and do no screening.
- Laptop or computer cameras should stay on throughout the workday so managers can see employees.

As I read these things, to say that I was shocked would be an understatement. These kinds of rules are infantile. Should employees raise their hand and request a hall pass to go pee too?

But this is the management thinking that has prevailed. This is Taylorism at its height. Monitor people. Make sure they are staying in line. Be certain that you are getting the most out of them.

When the purpose of business gets derailed from being a service to people into being a numbers game, this is the kind of thing that happens. Employees become tools, a means to an end, *things* to be managed. And as my friend learned, no creativity or initiative needed.

"One eye sees, the other feels."
-Paul Klee

Sidelining human concerns

Imagine you are a soldier wounded on a battlefield. You cry out for help. A medic comes and bandages your wounds, gets the bleeding under control, and gives you some pain relief. Then, they move on leaving you stressed out, wondering how long you'll lay there, and whether you'll be okay.

Now imagine an alternate version. You cry out for help. The medic comes, bandages you up, manages the bleeding, and helps with your pain. But this time, they stay with you. They assure you that you'll be okay. They promise to get you through this.

Which one would you rather have, Medic A or Medic B?

I've presented this scenario more times than I can count and never have I had anyone say they would rather have Medic A.

Who wants to be left alone? Who is okay with just having the medical matter taken care of while your emotional state is disregarded?

The idea here came out of a conversation with a friend who was a Navy corpsman—the Navy version of medic. He told me that in his corpsman training it was relayed many times that they were to always consider health and comfort. Health being the objective, medical, technical domain and comfort being the subjective, emotional, human domain. My friend said they made it abundantly clear that both domains were critical to caring for the wounded.

And this is not just a medical or military thing, this dual-domain model of human experience is present all around us.

Imagine a restaurant where the food is great but the servers have bad attitudes. Objectively, it's good. But subjectively? Not so much.

Think about the number of times you have called a contact center where the representative is nice and cordial but it is obvious they really don't know much technically about the product. From an objective, knowledge and skill perspective not great, but subjectively, on the human interaction side of things, no problems.

And it's not just present in human interactions. Our experience with things can demonstrate it too.

Ever heard of a Norman door?

The term comes from an observation made by Don Norman, the founding father of human-centered design, and it is something most of us have experienced. It describes a door that has a handle on both sides yet one side is push and the other is pull and it is not apparent. Functionally, it works, but it is not friendly to the user because one side of the door works against their intuitive sense. It looks like pull, but it is really push. The designer went for aesthetics rather than practicality.

Another everyday favorite of mine is the mayonnaise jar. Just below the cap, it tapers out to the wider portion of the jar. Due to the angle of the taper, it is impossible to get the last bits of mayonnaise. No implement, not a spoon or knife, can get into that tight angle. It's a bad design. It may look nice but it isn't practical. It makes me wonder if anyone at the mayonnaise company has ever used the jar.

The point here is this. Because the business world generally does not see everything it does in the light of service, it often sidelines human concerns. It does not view things from the human perspective. It has become Medic A. It has over-indexed on technical competence at the expense of human competence.

Case in point. In 2010, researchers found that average corporate training dedicates 72% of its resources on objective, technical skills and only 28% on subjective, human skills. And that figure is mirrored in the curriculums of business schools where 80% is objective and only 20% is subjective.

Ironically, in a 1918 joint study conducted by Harvard and Stanford, it was found that 85% of workplace success is due to subjective, human skills and only 15% due to objective, technical skills. And in a 2008 Google study called Project Oxygen, those early findings were supported when it was found that the top characteristics of Google's most successful employees were all human skills while technical skills came dead last.

Yet, here we are, over 100 years since that 1918 study with current evidence in full support, and we are still training people in reverse proportions with the lion's share going to technical skills.

This quote from Dr. Peter Pronovost at Johns Hopkins sums up the problem, "When I was in medical school, I spent hundreds of hours looking into a microscope—a skill I never needed to know or ever use. Yet I didn't have a single class that taught me communication or teamwork skills—something I need every day I walk into the hospital."

Why are we so stuck on the objective realm? Why, even though we know there is success to be found in considering the subjective domain, are we obsessed with the objective side? Well, it is most likely due to the fact that technical, tangible things are easy to measure. And humans love to measure things. We believe more when there are numbers. We trust what we can touch. Think about profit and productivity, both easy to measure. And both loved by business.

But there is a cost to this; it's hard to measure, but there is a cost nonetheless. Neglecting or disregarding the subjective domain can be perilous because it is the combination of those easy-to-measure, objective competencies *with* the subjective, emotional factors that impact customer perceptions. And those perceptions have a definite impact on whether they want to do business with you. I had a personal experience that gave me the opportunity to see this firsthand.

One summer, my wife and I got the crazy idea to take on a quite daunting home renovation project in order to help an elderly friend who needed to sell their house. As it turned out, we both acted as project managers and sometime contractors. During the project, we had four particular experiences with sub-contractors who provided various services. Each was distinct and each demonstrated different combinations of these subjective and objective domains.

Early in the project, once we had removed two walls and torn out everything in the kitchen and bathrooms, we needed electrical work done. Because our elderly friend had a longstanding relationship with an electrical contractor, we gave them a call. The electrician came and looked at everything, went over all that had to be done—largely a complete rewire to get the house up to building and safety codes—and gave us a cost estimate. He was very knowledgeable and made it apparent the he knew his stuff. My only misgiving was that he was a bit arrogant and did not like any questioning of his thinking. Nevertheless, he got the job.

The electrical work got done and all to a high standard, however, the electrician, as I feared, was irritating. He liked making his thoughts known whenever possible. For example, whenever we had an idea, he had one that was better. When he saw us working on something, he knew a better way. It was not pleasant and my wife and I were glad when he had finished.

So, when I got to thinking about the subjective and objective domains, while technically highly skilled, our electrician's selfish and uncooperative human skills found him lacking. This was something my wife and I found very frustrating.

The next experience involved repairing the countless holes the electrician had cut in walls for feeding wires through the house. Instead of trying to do all this patching ourselves, we decided it best to bring in someone skilled with drywall. With a bit of luck, a colleague of my wife's recommended a contractor to do it.

As it turned out, this contractor and her team were the nicest and most flexible people we worked with over the entire project, however, what they lacked was attention to detail. The work they did was not that good. There were a lot of little things missed. For example, they left several spots in need of sanding. There were holes around electrical outlets that were not patched well. There were just a lot of little inaccuracies. And while this contractor scored high on the subjective scale, they lacked on the objective scale, and this left me and my wife disappointed. You see, they were so unselfish and nice that we really wanted to be able to recommend them to others, but alas, we could not.

As we progressed through this project, one thing I never anticipated was how many times we would be running to the hardware store. It seems we constantly needed more lumber, nails, screws, and paint—lots of paint—not to mention cabinets and appliances. And since, it would seem, there were no standard measurements for anything back in the 1950s when the house was built, we had to buy things, see if they fit, and then take them back when they didn't. On one of these trips to return things, I had a memorable experience —albeit memorable for the wrong reasons.

With receipts in hand and products loaded on a cart, I made my way into the hardware store and stood in line. There were two employees handling returns. On my left was one who looked every bit like she had full command of her work while on my right was a young lady who looked far less motivated and much less in control.

As luck—or maybe bad luck—would have it, I was ushered to the young lady on the right. I stepped up and handed her the receipts for the returns. She took them, did a little perusal, and typed a couple of things into her computer. With that complete, she then took a scanning gun over to a couple of the large items and looked for barcodes so she could scan them into the system. In her sheepish yet abrupt style, she let me know that she had to do this because the items were not listed correctly on the receipt. When she couldn't find the barcodes, she went back to her counter and called for members of two different departments to come and identify a couple of items.

While she did that, I began looking over the receipts. I found both items and then went over and found two large barcode stickers on them that contained stock numbers which were exactly the same numbers as the ones on the receipts. I then alerted her to these discoveries to which she responded that she needed someone else to make sure this was right, so she sat and waited … quietly. Which of course meant I had to wait.

Eventually, someone came to the rescue and typed in all the correct numbers quickly and efficiently while the young lady at the counter watched.

You have probably guessed by now that my subjective-objective perceptions of the experience were not good. On the objective, technical side, the score was low—very low—because it was pretty obvious that my struggling young lady didn't know what she was doing, and on the subjective, human side, things were not much better. All in all, being low in both domains left me angry. In fact, when everything was completed and I left the counter, all I could think was, *how does this person have a job? Why do companies put someone who can't do the job properly and are not particularly good with people out in front? It never ceases to amaze me.*

Now, I will admit, I did not know everything about this young lady. She may have been having a bad day, or, more likely, was new to the job and needed more, and better, training. But it illustrates two things, 1) how an organization can do the wrong thing by putting someone in a place where they are likely to fail whether due to lack of ability, poor human skills, or both, and 2) how customers can rather ruthlessly react when their experience of the objective *and* subjective dimensions is poor.

After this less than satisfactory experience came my last sub-contracted work which involved getting new flooring for the kitchen, family room, and powder room. As the rooms were connected, the work would be a piece of cake for experienced flooring installers because they would be laying the same wood laminate flooring throughout. When the gentlemen arrived to do the job, I made a special request. I asked if they would mind installing the baseboard molding. I had purchased the material and figured that if they were laying the floor, it would be easy for them to just cut and install it at the same time to save me a job. Their response? "No problem at all." Pleasantly surprised that I didn't have to do any kind of song and dance to persuade them, I left them to it.

When I came back later that day, they had finished, and it was beautifully done. But there was more, they noticed that there was a sink and cabinet outside the powder room. Taking some initiative, they centered the cabinet under the mirror that hung there—the obvious place for it given the water pipes coming out of the wall beneath it—and cut molding precisely to accommodate that placement. When I saw that, I almost cried. They had taken yet another job off my plate and they did it without me even asking. These guys were amazing.

As far as the objective/subjective balance, with high quality work and a proactive "yes" attitude, they scored high in both. To say my wife and I were happy would be an understatement, we were ecstatic and have since recommended this company to anyone we know who needs flooring.

So, four experiences, each with different combinations of the subjective and objective elements that generated different reactions. When we experienced the high competence of our electrician, we were initially happy, but his overall self-focused, difficult attitude left us frustrated. With the drywall contractor, while their unselfish friendliness was welcome, their poor work left us disappointed. And in the product return experience at the hardware store, we were left angry due to the lack of both subjective care and objective ability. The only experience that was positive in every way was the flooring installers who, due to their unselfish kindness and flexibility as well as the high quality of the work, left us overjoyed.

If we look at the following chart, it sums up these four experiences.

At this point it should be plainly apparent, both the objective, technical concerns *and* subjective, human concerns have an impact, and just because the subjective ones are hard or even impossible to measure doesn't mean they are any less important.

One of my favorite movie quotes is from the film Dead Poets Society, and it speaks directly to this issue.

> *"We don't read and write poetry because it's cute. We read and write poetry because we are members of the human race. And the*

human race is filled with passion. And medicine, law, business, engineering, these are noble pursuits and necessary to sustain life. But poetry, beauty, romance, love, these are what we stay alive for." -John Keating

This, in so many words, says everything about why our over-indexing on the measurable things is flawed.

When we neglect the human side of life, we become less than human. We neglect what makes life worth living. We take away instead of adding.

Science helps us live, but art is why we live. The business world needs to get a much better appreciation of this.

Chapter 5

What Do We Do?

*"If you do not change direction, you may
end up where you are heading."*
-Lao Tzu

Before we see about changing the narrative, let's
look at what we have learned.

First, the magic bullet for great service is giving a
$#!+, a.k.a., the willingness to be inconvenienced by
the work of helping others, i.e., service. And the
reason it is the magic bullet is because this
willingness is what enables the action of serving, it is

the metaphorical game kickoff, first pitch, downbeat, name your figure of speech for getting things underway. However, for as many times as we find people and organizations who have this willingness and then demonstrate compassionate action like those above-and-beyond flight attendants, we find even more who, like the florist, don't have it and don't deliver.

So, why is giving a $#!+ the exception rather than the rule? Because we have been led and taught to believe that humanity is fundamentally selfish and competitive and that that is how we succeed. And nowhere do we see the impact of this thinking more than our workplaces. By prioritizing profit over people, managing over leadership, and technical concerns over human ones, business has, in so many ways, become the standard bearer for competition and self-interest.

But what of the second question that was posed back at the end of Chapter 2? Is it possible to make giving a $#!+ and the compassionate actions it spawns more of the rule instead of an exception? As I said when we first posed this, I believe the answer is yes. But this of course presents another question. What do we need to do?

Well, we need to change the narrative. We need to make service a noble calling. We need to inspire people to see that success is and has been better achieved through cooperation and helpfulness than through selfishly competing for personal gain. And, if we truly want make our workplaces and buying spaces better, we must restore the true purpose of our work to being about helping people achieve their goals rather than simply maximizing the organization's profits.

And in a perfect world, this would be easy. We would just preach the message, people would hear, and change would happen. Amen. But we don't live in a perfect world. We live with skeptics and cynics and firm believers in dog-eat-dog-world thinking. For them, service is just a role, business is all about money, people must be managed, and what gets measured is what matters.

All in all, it's not a breeding ground for service, and definitely not one for proactive, flexible, compassionate service. In fact, in too many places, service is barely in the conversation. It's an afterthought. It's a bolt-on. It's a necessary evil.

So, you may wonder, with all of these obstacles, why am I so sure it is possible to make a change and, if it is possible, how do we do it? This is our next stop.

PART TWO: TURNING IT AROUND

Chapter 6

It Can Be Done

"No enterprise can exist for itself alone. It ministers to some great need, it performs some great service, not for itself, but for others; or failing therein, it ceases to be profitable and ceases to exist."
-Calvin Coolidge

When I talk about businesses making service the central focus of their work, I typically get an oh-brother-here-we-go-more-unicorns-and-rainbows roll of the eyes followed by statements like, "we're not a charity, we are a for-profit organization" or "that's nice to talk about but it doesn't really work in the real world." Well, it's not some idealistic fantasy. You can still profit—and potentially make even more profit—and it can work in the real world. I know. I have experienced it.

I once attended a seminar being held at a hotel in south Florida where the giving-a-$#!+ mentality was in full bloom.

The day before the seminar, after getting checked in and set up in my room, I made my way to the beach for a walk before dinner. It was there that I met Lynn, the beach concierge. As I had never heard of a beach concierge before, I asked her about it. She explained that the position came from seeing beach-going guests being forced to go to the lobby of the hotel— a fair distance from the beach to see the hotel concierge whenever they had questions, needed information, or wanted tickets for an event or reservations to a restaurant. As she saw it, this was just painful and not great service. So, she went to the

General Manager of the hotel, explained the issue, and pitched the idea of a beach concierge. The General Manager loved it, created a position, and gave her the job.

To say Lynn was fantastic, would be an understatement. She was kind, welcoming, and full of local knowledge. She gave me some great tips on sites to look for during my walk, and also offered to help me find the right place for dinner upon my return.

True to her word, as I made my way back to the hotel, there was Lynn with menus in hand for restaurants both on and off property. She wanted to give me every possible option for a great dinner. As I had been traveling most of the day, I chose to stay on property. With that, Lynn made my reservation and I was set.

At dinner, my server was equally service focused. She made great suggestions and let me know I could sample anything if it would help me make a decision. While sampling a few things was tempting, I passed and gave her my order.

Very soon after though, she returned to my table with an appetizer in hand—I hadn't ordered an appetizer. She placed it on the table explaining that they had run out of the dish I ordered and that the appetizer was her way of apologizing. I told her that, while very kind, her gesture was appreciated but really not necessary. Running out of things happens, it certainly was not her fault and not a big deal so I asked for another suggestion and reordered. The rest of the meal went perfectly.

After dinner, I wanted to prepare for the morning by finding the location of my meeting room so I made my way to the lobby. After locating the large electronic hotel map, I started my search. No sooner had I got my bearings when a bellman came and asked if he could help. I asked him about the room and he gave me easy directions and even offered to walk me there if I wanted to see it. While a thoughtful gesture, I declined and thanked him.

When I went back to my room, I was greeted by a delightful gift on a small table just inside the doorway. Situated on a blue plate with a small portion covered in brown sugar were several chocolate turtles. It was a simulated beach scene. It was art. It was amazing, thoughtful, and creative, a quantum leap from the typical chocolates on the pillow.

The next morning, I took the elevator down to grab a quick breakfast and get to my seminar. When I stepped into the lobby, there were people everywhere checking in and out, going to meetings, and getting breakfast. To manage the chaos and ensure guests were well served, there were hotel employees from every corner of the operation giving directions, helping with luggage, valeting cars, and assisting the front desk.

It is noteworthy that this teamwork involved not only front-of-house employees but back-of-house employees and managers including the General Manager. And it wasn't just a morning thing, it happened throughout the day. Whenever guest traffic was busy, all hands were called to action. It was an amazing display of teammates helping to ensure not only guest success but teammate success.

Everything about this experience was outstanding. As a guest, I felt welcomed, wanted, and cared for. It was, as they say, the way it should be.

So, what happened here? What did they do?

Well, as you may have guessed, everyone and everything demonstrated giving a $#!+. There was a willingness to be inconvenienced.

The General Manager was willing to be inconvenienced to hear an idea and implement something that might add a cost.

Lynn was willing to be inconvenienced to approach guests, make connections, provide answers, share information, and take care of people.

A restaurant server was willing to be inconvenienced to make an apology with a gift.

A bellman was willing to be inconvenienced to walk over and offer assistance even though there was an automated option available.

Someone in housekeeping was willing to be inconvenienced to make chocolates on the pillow more than chocolates on the pillow.

And an entire team was willing to be inconvenienced to leave their regular work to help guests and fellow teammates.

Moreover, it appeared that everyone was willing to be inconvenienced to anticipate needs and be proactive. It was as if everything was thought out beforehand. Someone was there before I had to ask. Think about Lynn on the beach and the bellman in the lobby. I didn't go to them, they came to me. They were willing to go out of their way. Lynn came to me when we first met. She made her way from the comfort of her nicely shaded beach hut to come and say hello. And when I came back from my walk, she spied me down the beach and came toward me with menus in hand. Then, after dinner, the bellman saw me looking at the reader board and walked across the lobby to see if he could help. They went first. They inconvenienced themselves to help.

All in all, it appeared that everyone and everything in this hotel was centered on a willingness to be inconvenienced to be of service.

But why did they do it and what made it work and work consistently? Well, I got one clue when I was checking out.

While my receipt was being printed, I mentioned to the front desk agent how great the service was and she let me in on a secret. She said every day they had a brief stand-up meeting where all they talk about is service. In fact she said service was pretty much all that was talked about in any meeting. What was going right, what was going wrong, and how they could make it better were constant topics.

So, the more I thought about the impact of this practice on the staff as well as the things I had observed, the more clarity I got on what was clicking to make things work so well.

1. Everyone was on board with the idea that what they did was service. It had been made the organization's priority by being regularly stressed in meetings.
2. Throughout the organization, people were leading by example.

3. When teamwork was needed, teamwork happened. Team members served each other as much as customers.

4. Human concerns were included in everything:

   - Lynn saw that making guests go inside to ask questions, get a reservation, get tickets, etc. was not helpful, she thought about how to make it friendlier to beach-going guests.

   - The restaurant server did more than functionally apologize, she made it friendly with a gracious gift.

   - The bellman did not simply rely on an automated system to provide directions, he made a human connection to make it easier.

   - The housekeeper took chocolates on the pillow from fulfilling a corporate standard to delivering art.

- The entire team made taking care of people more important than their "day jobs."

From these observations, I have developed a model with actionable steps that any organization, team, department, work group, or even individual can employ to deliver value and give life to giving a $#!+.

- ALIGN around service as the priority
- LEAD by example
- SERVE everywhere
- put CARE in everything

We will look at these steps in more detail momentarily, but to understand how they work together, we need to first review something just about every one of us experienced as a child.

GIVING A $#!+

Chapter 7

The System

"A good system shortens the road to the goal."
-Orison Swett Marden

Did your parents teach you to say please and thank you? Mine did.

The training started with them telling me what they expected. "When you ask for something, say please. When you receive something, say thank you."

And the messaging wasn't just a one-time thing. Whenever I was in a situation where I should say please or thank you and didn't do it, I heard their favorite words, "what do you say?" And if I didn't want to get in big trouble, my next words had best be please or thank you.

Then, to keep up a constant parade of reminders, they demonstrated the behaviors themselves. Every time they asked for something or received something, out came please or thank you.

Essentially, my parent's method was to regularly message and model the expectation so it would be ever present in my mind and thus, hopefully, result in the desired action.

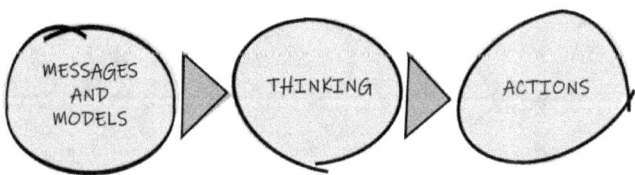

And this messaging and modeling was not just for me. My brothers, even though they were older and had been through the treatment already, got the "what do you say?" as much as I did. It was ongoing.

It was also not limited to our family. When I had a friend over for a sleepover or they joined us for dinner, if they asked for something and didn't say please, my dad would launch into, "In this family, we say please when we ask for something and thank you when we get something." From there, my friends had best say please and thank you or they would hear, "What do you say?" just like me and my brothers.

Essentially, my parents created a culture, a family culture. And when you ask people what culture means, you will often hear something like "how we do things around here" which is, if you think about it, what my parents were trying to do, they were trying to establish how our family did things.

But this "way of doing things" can be a blessing and a curse because the way the culture does things becomes what people think and do without thinking. And if those are good things, it's a blessing, but if they are not-so-good things, it's a curse.

For example, if my dad had walked around the house regularly using offensive language and making racist comments and I never heard anything telling me that this was unacceptable behavior, what do you guess my actions would look like outside our house? Well, without thinking, because it had become a reflex, I would probably have used offensive language and made racist comments—at least until I got yelled at enough or beat up or thrown in jail.

And while that example was fiction, we can see a non-fiction example of this same principle having an impact on our schools. Think how often students hear things like, "Getting into a good college or getting a good job requires getting good grades." When we send this message over and over it tells students that the purpose of school is less about learning and more about getting high scores. It creates a mindset where "is this going to be on the test?" and memorization take precedence over understanding and knowledge. And it inspires behaviors that include taking the easiest classes, doing the minimum necessary, and even cheating. Thus, by repeatedly communicating a misguided message, we have turned schools into places where regurgitation of content is more important than application of concepts resulting in bad behavior being unwittingly encouraged.

In a similar way, we have done damage to our workplaces. With the regular messaging of money, money, money, bottom-line this and bottom-line that coupled to leadership that prioritizes productivity for profit, cutting costs no matter the impact, laying people off to make the balance sheet look better, and treating people uncivilly in order to maintain authority, a way of thinking gets created that equates success to money, getting promotions, and staying ahead of coworkers. And that thinking inspires behaviors that range from doing "good enough" work and cutting corners to lying and cheating.

What we hear regularly—what's messaged—and what we see regularly—what's modeled—influences how we think which drives the actions we take. And when the message is broadly communicated in an organization, a collective consciousness begins to form. And when the collective consciousness becomes what people do without thinking, a culture develops. And culture is what drives the actions that are experienced by customers, investors, and the general public.

Each of the steps in the Align-Lead-Serve-Care model we introduced in the last chapter plays a part in this Messaging-Modeling-Thinking-Action process.

Aligning people to service as a priority happens with the right messaging and it gets modeled when leaders commit to being examples. When combined, those elements build a cultural habit-of-thought that encourages people to help others inside and outside the organization with caring actions that consider human concerns as much as technical ones.

So, here's a big question, what culture do you want? What kind of actions do you want your customers to experience? If it's a spirit of giving a $#!+, it all begins with the messages communicated.

"The highest of distinctions is service to others."
-King George VI

Messages (Aligning to Service as Priority)

If you have ever been in a back hallway at a Ritz Carlton hotel, you have seen the words "We are Ladies and Gentlemen serving Ladies and Gentlemen" either on a poster or painted on a wall or both. This is the Ritz Carlton motto, and if you are an employee, it is something that you cannot avoid. You see it and hear it regularly and often.

On your first day, you are handed a card for your wallet or pocket. The card is printed with the company's Credo, Employee Promise, Three Steps of Service, 12 Service Values, and, yes, the Motto. It is meant to be an ever-present companion and reminder of the company's chief priority, service.

Additionally, each day before every shift in every Ritz Carlton hotel and office around the world, much like the hotel in my south-Florida experience, employees attend a 10-minute lineup meeting. These meetings serve a three-fold purpose: 1) affirmation of service as the company's priority, 2) celebration of great service performance, and 3) communication of news, problems, and solutions. Yet another reminder of what matters most.

It is worth mentioning here that at Ritz Carlton, service isn't just about serving customers, it's about serving co-workers within the organization as well. Everyone, customers and co-workers alike, is included in the phrase "ladies and gentlemen." Consequently, respecting and helping teammates is as important as respecting and helping guests. This is why everyone gets a wallet card and has service-focused lineup meetings. Service is not just an expectation for some, it is an expectation for everyone.

Clearly, if you want your organization to serve well, you need to make it the priority, and it needs to be apparent in the messaging to every employee. "We serve. That is what we do. And it's not about *who* you serve but *that* you serve—throughout the organization and beyond."

By communicating this kind of service-first message regularly and often, you align everyone. You get the entire crew in your boat rowing together. They know what matters most, and based on that, make decisions from a service perspective.

Consistent and persistent messaging is the first step to making your organization one that gives a $#!+.

TIPS FOR MAKING IT HAPPEN

- Develop a service-first motto or rally cry of your own and start messaging it regularly and often.
- Start meetings by talking about service. Read customer comments, recognize employees who have been acknowledged by customers,

go over customer-survey results, or have a frontline employee come in and tell you where they see customer challenges. Make it clear, helping people is the first agenda item in the meeting because it is the first agenda item for the company.

- Hold pre-shift lineup meetings. Use the Ritz Carlton meeting format of affirmation, celebration, and communication as a template. Do this, 10 minutes, every day.

"Imagine for yourself a character, a model personality, whose example you determine to follow, in private as well as in public."
-Epictetus

Models (Leading by Example)

I am sure you've heard the old saying, "do as I say, not as I do." And hopefully, you are aware that it describes a very ineffective tactic because it's not aligned to what humans naturally tend to do. Most people tend towards imitating what they *see* leaders do rather than blindly doing what they *say* to do.

Imitation is a big part of how we humans operate. We are endowed with what are known as mirror neurons that help us copy what we see. While the jury is out on exactly why this is so, many scientists believe it came about as a survival mechanism.

Imagine a young child of our prehistoric ancestors. When they saw mom doing something and it kept her safe, fed, and alive, they imitated it. And because language was not yet a reality, and survival was pretty important, imitation as a learning tool became a necessity. And it has not disappeared over the centuries, we still see it today. Go over to a baby and stick out your tongue. After just a few times, the baby will copy you and stick out their tongue in response.

And while imitation has proven useful and helped us survive, it is also something that torments parents the world over. It is so easy to fall into the trap of telling children to do or not do something and then do something ourselves that counters all of that.

I remember once, in the pre-GPS era, while driving my kids to some sporting event, I was a bit lost and searching for the right road to turn on. In the heat of the moment, I said a few choice words. Within seconds, my daughter was keen to let me know that I had told her and her brother to never use such bad language and that I was now breaking the rules—it was a humbling lesson to say the least.

Somehow, the gods of good parenting spoke to me and prevented me from telling her to be quiet. Instead, I stopped the car, turned around in my seat and told my daughter that she was right and I was wrong. I told her to call me out on this anytime— she's had to do this many times since— because the rules apply to me as much as her and her brother.

If I had reacted differently and simply carried on, it would have given my kids a ticket to do whatever they liked. I can see it now. My children cursing like sailors at school and on the playground. Shocked, angry parents telling their children to avoid those bad-mouthed kids. And before you know it, none of my offspring are welcome for play dates.

This makes it abundantly clear how critical leader behaviors are to follower behaviors. If expectations are to move past words on a page, it is up to leaders to provide the example. They must walk the talk. They must be models for imitation.

However, every day in our workplaces, business leaders demand that their employees treat customers with care, react with urgency, and go to extremes to be helpful, yet treat those same employees in uncivil ways, do not respond with any sense of timeliness, and make almost no effort to be helpful. Then they wonder why customers complain about rudeness, lack of urgency, and indifference.

Thus, the power of modeling in the workplace cannot be understated. Leader behaviors can have an inordinate impact both inside and outside the workplace.

Case in point. On my first day working in the hotel industry, I met my new manager, Jorge. And after talking over some details about scheduling and general expectations, he told me I needed to learn my way around and meet some of the hotel staff. So, we went for a walk.

Walking with Jorge that morning was an eye opener. At every possible opportunity, an expected behavior was demonstrated and instruction given. Every person, whether hotel guest or hotel employee was greeted with a smile to which Jorge piped in, "If you treat everyone like a customer, you will always deliver great service." Every scrap of paper, candy wrapper, dropped coffee stirrer, anything looking like trash was picked up and placed in a garbage can followed by the words, "This is our hotel and it should look as great as your home." And whenever anyone remotely looked like they needed help, Jorge would say, "We are here to help people no matter who they are," so we offered our services.

We did similar walks like this on many an occasion and I will never forget these prescient words. "The more you do these service practices, the more they will become habits, and the more they become habits, you will find yourself doing them everywhere, not just at work. You will find yourself naturally helping people with groceries at the store, holding doors, greeting people on the street, service will become a reflex." Well, his theory was spot on. The more I followed his example, the more I did those things, and as for doing them in my personal life, he was right again.

So, be mindful of my experience. Driving giving-a-$#!+ service behaviors is not something that can be relegated to a team meeting with a PowerPoint presentation and a hearty "now go make it happen" speech. And if you are thinking additional training or overhauling hiring practices will do it, they will not, at least not for the long haul. If you want to bring about long-lasting change, expected behaviors must be consistently modeled by management. And when they become habits, all the benefits, over time, will come to life for both those inside and outside the organization.

TIPS FOR MAKING IT HAPPEN

- Give people a sense that they matter. Consider people's lives, cares, and concerns. See those around you as people with hopes, fears, and problems just like you.

- Listen more. People want to be seen, heard, and understood. Whether every idea is acted on is not as important as the respect shown. Moreover, pay particular attention to your customers and frontline employees to learn more about what changes or improvements might be needed. You will learn a lot by simply listening.

- Ask questions. Being invited to give a point of view is empowering. It gives people a needed sense of importance in the overall success of the operation. When they feel their ideas matter, it boosts ownership, and ownership boosts diligence in getting things done.

- Build trust by transparently delivering information honestly and simply. Treating employees as adults by giving them the true state of things both good and bad encourages optimism rather than pessimistic cynicism.

- Foster a practice of solving problems collaboratively. This builds teamwork and camaraderie which will spread out to customers.

- Empower and encourage team members to be creative and resourceful. When change or new ideas are needed, instead of pulling a committee of leaders together, include many levels of employees to develop and implement solutions.

- Pursue excellence. Find little ways to improve your performance each and every day. Write better, listen better, help better, be better. Your discipline and quiet diligence will inspire.

- Keep your eyes open and your fingers on the pulse of your workplace. Work to create an environment where people want to perform at their best.

"There is no higher religion than human service. To work for the common good is the greatest creed."
-Woodrow Wilson

Thinking (A Serving-Everywhere Culture)

Somebody once sent me a humorous picture that showed the painted line on the shoulder of a road running around a downed tree. Essentially, instead of moving the tree, the painters just went around it. Although it was funny, it was also disturbing. The more I looked at the picture, the more I thought about the "it's not my job" thinking of those painters. It got me thinking about silos and the cultures that give rise to them.

Silos, the thinking that my department or job must be successful regardless of how it affects others, is a damning thing in business. When employees begin to do only what is in their job description or only what helps them or their department reach their exclusive goals, it stifles collaboration and any sense of teamwork.

The ironic thing is that management is often where silos start. When competition is promoted and sticks and carrots are used as motivators, a message is sent that selfish performance is necessary.

A good example is sports teams that incent players to reach certain individual performance goals. We've all seen it when a basketball player begins to hog the ball and shoot whenever they get the chance because, if they make a certain number of points, they get a bonus. The problem with this is that it often works in opposition to the team winning consistently. The carrot may work for the individual but it is a stick to the team.

And while competition is not inherently bad, it is usually a detriment to teamwork because it is inherently divisive. It supports a zero-sum game with winners and losers. It is hard to build unity when one person triumphs while all the others fail.

Collaboration, on the other hand, is all about moving collectively as a strong unit to cross the finish line and win together. When you give everyone a common goal as a focus and then encourage collaborating creatively to achieve it, you break down silos and enable your business to meet the increasingly demanding needs of today's business world.

Thus, to be a great team, you must work together and share. If one department needs help and another can spare people, money, or expertise, they share for the good of the whole. If one person needs help, others run to the rescue, for the good of the whole.

But for that to happen, the collective thinking needs to center around each team member looking after and helping the team member next to them. This means managers helping employees to help each other to help customers.

The problem though is that most businesses don't think this way. They talk about caring for customers but rarely talk about coworkers caring for coworkers. They talk about service for those outside the company but rarely about service for those inside it. But why? Why do business leaders expect people to get in front of customers and provide great service with a happy smile but have no expectation for that same thing from coworker to coworker? It's absurd.

And here's a critical consideration, employees simply cannot help customers most effectively outside the house if they aren't helping each other effectively inside the house. What's accepted and practiced inside is what will get practiced outside.

When we create environments where employees are encouraged to serve each other and build each other up, and where their leaders do likewise and model those behaviors, we can only expect that that mindset, that thinking, that collective consciousness, will influence how employees not only work in the office but with customers on the outside as well.

This is precisely why culture, that collective way-we-do-things-around-here thinking, is not just a buzzword, it is potentially the most important factor in consistently and successfully negotiating customer relationships. And it is these relationships that are really what your business is all about.

So, think about this. When things get tough and start going wrong inside your business, how do your people handle it? Do they rant and rave and blame each other, or do they help each other and find solutions together? What you see is the product of your culture. And you can bet that if they fight and blame each other, they do it with customers. But if you've created a culture of service to one another, you can bet on them doing that with customers instead.

125

Imagine your entire workforce trusting each other, communicating well, and rowing together to achieve a common result of customer success. Imagine people freely jumping in to be helpful. Imagine managers rolling up their sleeves to lend a helping hand to their team members and those team members helping each other without grumbling or complaining about who is or isn't pulling their weight. Imagine senior executives looking for ways to help employees by making the work easier and less complicated. Just imagine how much all of that helping would impact customers and how much it would just make life better.

When collaboration involves every department and employee at every level, it creates a workplace where everyone *wants* to be rather than *has* to be, and that better workplace can only translate to a better customer experience not to mention greater financial success.

So, how can we change the thinking inside of our house? What can we do to make things go differently? It begins with business leaders actively demonstrating and encouraging care for not only customers but for fellow teammates. It requires a new habit of thought in the organization where "How can I help?" becomes a standard mantra.

While a competitive work environment may drive results, it does so with fear-based methods that encourage individualism and divisiveness. Whereas collaborative, service-focused environments drive results by way of teamwork and cooperation.

TIPS FOR MAKING IT HAPPEN

- Change the conversation. Make it clear daily that it's not important who crosses the finish line first, it's important that the organization crosses it as a whole.
- Foster collaboration by bringing representatives from different teams together

as much as possible. For example, when the sales department needs to come up with ways to present a new product to customers, have people from, say, manufacturing, operations, marketing, and the shipping department join the discussion. You will get views and ideas that may diverge greatly from what your sales team sees all the time.

- Give your team members many tools to connect. With people working remotely from far-flung parts of the company map, the more tools for easily holding cross-functional dialogue at virtually any time, the better.

- Serve those around you. If you want the organization to deliver value to customers, everyone inside the organization needs to deliver value to each other—and that begins with you.

- Encourage a team approach. Break up silos by including cross-functional roles on projects. Have all-hands daily huddles to celebrate accomplishments and communicate problems. Get cross-functional input in solving problems. Ensure everyone begins to understand the impact of decisions on others. Get more people working together for the bigger goal of helping everyone succeed.

- In daily stand-up or lineup meetings, ask people to speak up if they need help. It will be slow at first but eventually people will begin asking. And don't be shy yourself, be the first to step up and talk about where you could use help. Once they see it is safe and not some admission of their weakness, people will reach out.

"Politeness and civility are the best capital ever invested in business. Large stores, gilt signs, flaming advertisements, will all prove unavailing if you or your employees treat your patrons abruptly. The truth is, the more kind and liberal a man is, the more generous will be the patronage bestowed upon him."
-P.T. Barnum

Actions (Putting Care in Everything)

Times are evolving from Industrial Age thinking to Digital Age thinking. Instead of seeing business as simply a means for getting products into the hands of needy customers, we are beginning to see it as more of a partnership to help people accomplish things. This means relationships are becoming more and more critical. And how people feel along the way is what can make or break these relationships.

As was discussed in Chapter 4, most organizations spend a lot of time ensuring that everything they do is technically excellent. They train, design, and set standards to be sure that they can get the job done efficiently and at a high level of quality. However, what gets neglected is how it all impacts humans. The question of how friendly things are to customers or employees is rarely asked.

Danny Meyer, the great restaurateur of Gramercy Tavern, Union Square Café, and Shake Shack fame, has great words on this in his book, Setting the Table, "It's remarkable to me how many businesses shine brightly when it comes to acing the tasks but emanate all the warmth of a cool fluorescent light. That explains how a four-star restaurant can actually attract far fewer loyal fans than a two- or three-star place with soul."

What this means to today's business leader is that they need to start thinking about the human-oriented, subjective dimension as much as the task-oriented, objective one. In other words, they should be considering not only *what* they deliver but *how* it is being delivered. They need to understand and make it clear that while successfully providing the functional, objective dimension is a must, it is just table stakes. The thing that will make the company stand out is by making everything it does friendly which means paying much more attention to the subjective dimension.

This means making human concerns not only part of person-to-person interactions, but part of every other vehicle used for value delivery. These include props—the products and environments, both brick-and-mortar and digital, that customers encounter—and processes—the workflows and procedures that are needed to conduct business. And while it is pretty easy to see how people can demonstrate the objective and subjective dimensions by being competent and kind, how, for example, do products, environments, and processes do it?

Although it may seem a stretch at first, products can demonstrate subjective, human concerns. They do it in their form and design. When a product is beautiful, elegant, and clean it is aesthetically pleasing which demonstrates thoughtfulness and caring. When its operation makes sense and does not require a huge learning curve, it is friendly. Put simply, any product that is attractive and does not require research to learn a series of complicated maneuvers to get things done will rank high on the subjective scale.

And as for the objective dimension, that is all about function. When a product works and does what it is supposed to do, consistently, that will get high marks on the objective scale.

The other prop, the environments where we experience businesses, can be seen in a similar way. Imagine a waiting room in an auto repair shop where the only things there are hard plastic chairs. While it is objectively functional—there are chairs to sit on—it scores low on the subjective, human scale—it's not comfortable or pleasing in any way. But with the addition of some comfortable chairs, a TV on the wall, and some decent coffee, we go from being functional alone to being both functional and friendly.

It is no different with processes. When a process is easy and uncomplicated, it demonstrates kindness to the person entrenched in it. On the flip-side, when processes are difficult, well, you guessed it, they're unkind.

And as far as the objective dimension, processes must be effective, that is how they prove their ability. If you go all the way through a journey and really don't get what you want or need, the process is useless.

The following chart sums this up.

	OBJECTIVE	SUBJECTIVE
Props (products & places)	functional	friendly
Processes	efficient	easy
People	competent	kind

What we see here is how just about everything a business does can demonstrate not only an ability to get things done but care in doing it. Moreover, we can see an opportunity. It's an opportunity to make a mark. It's an opportunity for a business to show how they are different by considering the humans they interact with.

If giving a $#!+ is to truly come alive, organizations must be willing to be inconvenienced by the continual work required in balancing the objective and subjective dimensions of everything for all stakeholders, both customers and employees alike. As much as customers want friendly and functional products and places, easy and effective processes, and kind and competent people to deal with, so do employees. Get a handle on the experiences of all of the people who encounter your business both inside it and outside it and make adjustments to balance the dimensions. This can change the game like it did in my seminar-hotel experience.

TIPS FOR MAKING IT HAPPEN

Here are some questions business leaders should be regularly asking about the objective-subjective balance in each delivery system. Use these to begin getting your team members involved in finding ways to create more human-centered yet functional delivery systems throughout the organization.

- Is our product, the outcome we deliver to customers, beautiful and/or elegant in its unique way? Is it aesthetically pleasing in its look or beautifully hidden so as not to disturb the natural surrounding beauty? How can we make it more attractive?

- Does our product function the way it should? Are there hassles in using it? How often are there breakdowns?

- Are the places where customers encounter us, both brick-and-mortar and virtual, comfortable and easy to get around? Is the environment pleasing?

- Do those places serve their function well? Is everything that is needed in the right place? Does everything do the job it needs to do? Is anything not needed? Is anything additional needed?

- Are the processes we use difficult? How many steps are there? How many people must be involved? How many points of contact must the end user connect with? Does the end user have to repeat things?

- Are our processes effective? Do they result in success every time?

- Do our people demonstrate care and concern? Are they courteous and civil?

- Are our employees competent? Do they need training? Can they provide solutions?

Summary

Every company says they want to deliver great service and create better customer experiences. And many of them try very hard to make it happen, yet, despite all those well-intentioned attempts using training, complicated systems, and piles of data, they fall short. And they fall short because they are not addressing the fundamental challenges of profit-first mentality, people management, and the sidelining of human concerns.

The Align-Lead-Serve-Care model that we have just discussed is a way forward. With it and some give-a-$#!+ willingness, your organization can achieve its potential as a service leader and, ultimately, as a consistently successful business.

We leave this chapter with this brief summary of the model.

1. ALIGN to Service as Priority: Align everyone in the organization, team, or work group around service as the fundamental reason for existence. Make that the rally cry to unify everyone. Make service the first

thing on meeting agendas and communicate a service-first message in daily lineups.

2. LEAD by Example: Develop a leadership team that is of service to their teams, models cooperative, helpful behaviors, and inspires their team members to be of service.

3. SERVE Everywhere: Encourage a team approach where co-workers help each other. Break up silos by including cross-functional roles on projects. Get cross-functional input in solving problems, and ensure everyone considers the impact of decisions on others.

4. Put CARE in Everything: Continuously improve not only the technical effectiveness of products, processes, places, and people, but the human effectiveness as well.

Chapter 8

Making Change

"To desire and strive to be of some service to the world, to aim at doing something which shall really increase the happiness and welfare and virtue of mankind - this is a choice which is possible for all of us; and surely it is a good haven to sail for."
-Henry Van Dyke

The last chapter was largely a focus on a system, how it works, and how leaders can use it to make organizational change. And while I champion that and hope some will take heed and do it, it is more likely that change efforts will fall more to choir members than the choirmaster. However, you may now be thinking, *how can I possibly make an impact? I am not in a position to drive anything that significant.* Well, don't lose heart or enthusiasm. While you may not be one of the chief decision makers and you may see yourself as just one person who cannot change city hall, the transformation we are seeking to make often begins with individuals who, while perhaps not having authority, do have belief. They believe that service is critical to business success. They believe that their organization needs to up its service game or find itself behind the times. They believe they can make a difference and improve the lives of others. But how do they do it?

Back in 1984, there was a TV advertisement for Faberge shampoo where Heather Locklear famously "told two friends, and they told two friends, and they told two friends." This is how moving an organization can take shape. It may begin with your example influencing a couple of others who influence a few others and before you know it your team is working in a service-focused way. Maybe your team then influences other teams and again before you know it a department has made service-focused improvements. And so it goes, department to department until large parts of the organization are thinking and behaving in a service-focused way.

What's more, we can use the same Align-Lead-Serve-Care model we discussed for organizations.

I am going present this in two ways. First, we will explore some steps you can take in your personal behavior to begin your own service-excellence practice. Then, we will investigate how you can, if you choose, begin building a larger movement to influence change in your team, work group, department, or company.

Your Personal Service-Excellence Practice

Think about the work you do, is it for you or for someone else? Usually, it's the latter. Typically, most of us are providing value for coworkers, managers, or customers. And at home it's not much different. Think of those mundane chores around the house. You don't do most of them for you; you do them for your partner, spouse, or children. A vast majority of our lives is wrapped around service and we don't even recognize it. We bring value, sometimes in the smallest ways, on a daily basis. And much like dieting or physical exercise, an effective methodology for making this an even more predominant part of our lives is to create a practice.

My wife is a yogi, a keen, longtime practitioner and instructor of yoga. She does it every day, and she says the key to keeping it going and getting better at it is by doing it regularly, without fail, until it becomes something that you miss if you don't do it. You see, by "practicing" an activity or series of activities consistently over time, those activities become what you do without thinking. They become part of what we might call your own personal culture.

A great example of this comes from a comedian named Michael Jr. who, during his shows, tells a story about how he made a mindset shift that caused a change in routine that impacted his life and career forever. And in that change we can find parallels to the Align-Lead-Serve-Care model.

Early in his career, while waiting to go on stage for one of his shows, Michael Jr. found himself thinking about comedy and his reason for doing it. As he pondered, he had a flash of insight. He had always been led to believe success in comedy was about getting laughs. But this seemed off base. This made it sound like the audience was there for the comedian and that just didn't sound right. Shouldn't the comedian be there for the audience? This thought brought about a life-changing epiphany. What if, instead of trying to get laughs, he began instead, giving people opportunities to laugh? In other words, rather than approaching comedy with the thinking, "I am here to *get* something from people," approaching it with different thinking, "I am here to *give* something to people." While it might not sound earth shaking, it was.

This shift wasn't just a change in thinking, it was a fundamental change in purpose. Where once he was focused on a selfish motive of *getting* laughs, this new purpose focused on the service-centered motive of *giving* to others and improving their lives. This simple mindset shift inspired a new direction.

While signing autographs after this "epiphany," Michael Jr. spotted a homeless man across the street. He says that he had never seen a homeless person there before, not because the person had never been there, but because he had never been willing to be inconvenienced to notice. Now though, with this new-found, service-focused purpose, he saw the man and decided to give him an opportunity to laugh. He crossed the street and spent time with him. They talked, they shared, and they laughed. Michael Jr. made a difference, and that difference was born out of a focus on giving before any thought of getting.

From this experience, Michael Jr. has made it a regular habit to not only hold this service-centered, giving mindset during his shows but to demonstrate it in other places like homeless shelters, prisons, and safe houses for battered women and children to give people who rarely get opportunities to laugh, more opportunities than they can count. The shift from get to give changed Michael Jr.'s life as well as countless lives of others.

In addition, during his shows, it's not just about telling jokes. I have seen videos of him stopping during performances to have conversations with the audience on deep topics like living life with purpose. The performances are not just typical stand-up comedy, they are about connecting with and helping those in his audience. Thus, it is not just about the technical aspect of jokes, there is consideration for subjective, human connection that goes beyond the objective dimension alone.

So, what about Aligning, Leading, Serving, and Caring? How does Michael Jr.'s story correlate to that?

First, Michael Jr. has aligned to a kind of mantra, "instead of getting laughs, give people an opportunity to laugh." This leads him to regularly ask himself, "What can I *give* from myself?" rather than "What can I *get* for myself?" He then leads by example by doing it and talking about it. He also serves everywhere, not just on stage—his workplace—but in those shelters and prisons we talked about earlier. Finally, he makes his work about more than just jokes (the objective dimension), he makes it about impacting his audience in deeper ways (the subjective dimension).

So, getting back to what *you* can do, step one, as with Michael Jr., is to align yourself around service as your priority. Make your fundamental mindset giving rather than getting. Create a personal mantra of your own. Begin asking yourself every day, "What can I give and how can I help?"

Step two is to lead by example. Actively look for opportunities to help others, not to be a nuisance mind you, but to be an actual contributor to someone else's success. The opportunities are all around if you open your eyes. They can be as simple as opening the door for someone whose hands are full or as complicated as editing a major report for a coworker. It begins with the willingness to be inconvenienced and then awareness of your surroundings. As we learned from Daniel Goleman, we have to open our eyes and notice. If you are vigilant, you can find opportunities in many places to help those around you, and when you jump at the chance whenever possible, you lead the way and become a model.

The third step is to subtly inspire others to serve everywhere by helping them develop a service mindset. You get this started by recognizing their efforts. When someone is helpful to you, say something, give them a hearty "thank you," send an email, give them a handwritten note, just be grateful and let them know it. And when you see or hear about someone being helpful, recognize them. Let them know how important their helpfulness is to success. You don't have to go overboard, just a simple "I think the way you helped Susan was fantastic, I am inspired," will send the message. From there, oxytocin will do its job and begin prompting a more helpful community.

The final step is to better balance those objective and subjective dimensions we have discussed by continually improving how you deliver what you deliver. While you should always stay on top of your technical game by developing your skills and knowledge, you should also continually improve your human game by making the value you provide easy and hassle free. If you are delivering a report, for instance, make it easy to read and provide a key and directions. If you are making a schedule, make sure it accommodates everyone fairly and is easy to understand. The things you deliver need to be of service and make the lives of the recipients better, otherwise, it is just more of a pain and no one needs more pain. Think of the person or people you are helping and deliver the work for them that you would want delivered to you.

So, to recap, four steps, or to-dos, for developing your own personal service-excellence practice:

1. Align to service-first by cultivating a service-focused mindset with a mantra or mission statement that inspires you.
2. Lead by example by looking for and taking opportunities to be helpful.
3. Encourage serving everywhere by recognizing the helpfulness of others

4. Put care in everything by ensuring you deliver help that is not only functional but friendly.

Once you get settled practicing these service-focused habits of your own, you can, if you feel inclined and adventurous, do even more to grow a service-focused mindset throughout your organization. You can, if you feel inclined and adventurous, lead a movement.

Raise a Flag

It is likely that the executives and managers in your company believe they care enough about service and will see no need to do anything different. Thus, posting a manifesto on the boardroom door that speaks to the need for more focus on service will have no impact. In addition, it is probable that behind closed doors, those executives and managers who "care" only care to a point, as in, "Service is very important to this company... provided it doesn't interfere with sales, efficiencies, or the bottom line."

So, considering these realities, as a forward-thinking maverick who wants your company to thrive by moving its mindset to something more service focused, you must now start thinking about how to lead a grassroots movement. It is going to be a bottom-up effort.

And, while all of this may be giving you second thoughts, you need to get hold of yourself. Don't sell yourself short. Anyone, regardless of role, can bring about change, and it is change that moves organizations forward. And as we have shown, in this age where service and the experience it spawns is more and more critical, companies need to change their priorities to accommodate it. Thus, your company desperately needs your voice, whether it knows it or not. A few revolutionaries like you, willing to do the work of making the company more relevant to the times, is just the prescription the organization requires to evolve.

Developing a service-focused mindset in a company takes a lot of time and persistent effort. It may take months, but more likely, quarters or even years, and it will take more people than just you. Thus, you need to get some followers and doing that means being able to talk about it.

While you may know that the nature of the business world is changing, and that developing a cultural mindset focused on service is critical in response to that, others may not, so you need to be able to talk clearly about what service-focus means. Thus, you need to define it and become facile with why it is needed and how it can benefit the organization.

You can come up with your own definition or you can use mine. Here's how I put it: service focus is when an organization makes it a priority for employees to best serve each other inside the organization so they can best serve people outside of it.

This definition makes it clear that we are not aiming at a focus on customers, employees, or any other stakeholder, we are focusing on service itself because service is something necessary in our relationships with all. In other words, we want to focus on service because when everyone is serving everyone, every stakeholder benefits. In fact, even our products and processes benefit because service focus can drive innovation in making those things more helpful to all who use them.

So, armed with clear thinking on service focus and an ability to talk about it, your next move is to begin building a small change-army to create a movement.

Recruiting for this "army" means searching for others who feel like you do. This is not as tough as it may sound. There are far more people who care about such things than you might think. Just start looking and listening and before you know it some like-minded souls will rear their heads. And don't just head down to the Customer Support Department, that's the obvious haven of compatriots, you need to find allies in other departments, and they are there in Marketing, Sales, and HR to name a few, you just need to get going and seek them out.

All you need to do is get talking, and you will be amazed at the number of people who share your belief in the importance of and need for an overall service mindset to make the company more successful. So, get together over lunch. Keep in touch via text, email, or networking apps. Share ideas. Start a book club. Just build excitement and momentum for a change to a more helpful company. The more enthusiastic your believers, the better.

Okay, now that you have clarity on service focus and what you are trying to achieve as well as the backing of a new-found army of supporters, you need to get management interested.

But before we get going on this, you need to know, getting your management team to care about, not to mention invest in, a service-focused transformation is difficult, and here's why.

Every day executives and managers deal with all kinds of people pushing their ideas for innovation and improvement, and to each of them they have to say no. And they say no because they've been getting results with the status quo so there's no need to rock the boat.

Furthermore, because service is usually not at the top of the priority list, you will be starting with an added disadvantage. You will hear it in their words.

- "We have a customer service department, why do we need anything more?"
- "What do you mean? Our service is excellent."
- "Service is a cost; we don't need more cost."
- "What's wrong with our service? Our scores are good."
- "How will this help the bottom line?"

As you see, they will take any suggestion about making service a focus for the company as an unworthy business initiative. To them, business is a rough-and-tumble venture second only to warfare.

Of course, they are missing a few vital facts:

1. The business of business is all about people helping people. That means it is fundamentally about service. Thus, everything a business does should only be in service of that one larger purpose.
2. Without happy customers, businesses cannot reach their financial goals and cannot have long-lasting success.
3. Focusing on service does not have to cost more. In fact, some of the adjustments can actually lower costs.

Okay, but we still don't know how to move management to get on board.

You begin by having conversations. Whenever you get a chance to talk to executives and/or managers, do what you can to inspire them with a vison of what you see as the organization's potential. Communicate your belief in the value the business brings and how it truly helps people. Talk about how the business could make an even bigger impact by providing a better service experience.

If they get interested, discuss how the business world is finding itself in the midst of an overall cultural shift from an Industrial Age, product-centric, wealth-creation mindset to a Digital Age, service-focused, value-creation mindset, and how this shift is making the delivery of good service more critical than ever. Moreover, for organizations to consistently deliver good service to customers outside the organization, they must deliver it inside the organization as well. Thus, instead of so many other things being the company's priority, service needs to move into first place.

One final thing to think about is your tone. If management thinks all you are doing is whining and complaining, they will turn you off in a second. Hence, do not kick off your conversation with how bad things are. Instead, begin by talking about how much potential the organization has and how you really want to contribute to helping it get there. Have a plan in your back pocket that is simple and low cost, and present a logical, cogent argument. Here are some points to get started...

- We have so much potential but some of it is not being tapped.

- The business world is evolving to be more about experiences, and service is the linchpin in that. We must move to an aligned service strategy that encourages and supports executives being of service to managers who are of service to team members.

- Companies that focus on service do much better financially. If you want some proof, look at the performance of the leading companies on the American Customer

Satisfaction Index. Over the last 15 years, those top ACSI performers have generated a cumulative return in excess of 1,500% compared to the S&P 500 return of just over 400%. By making service a priority from management to team members, every team member, not just customer-facing ones, we can see those returns.

In closing, it is critical that you do not give up. This is an uphill battle, but quitting means the organization never moves forward, and not moving forward means either a plateau or maybe a slow death.

Face it, people don't like change, least of all managers, but our world is all about change, especially in this era of rapid innovation. Managers just fear tipping any balance the wrong way. They never like to diverge from what they have seen as tried and true. They typically have a hard time seeing evolution until it is staring them hard in the face.

So, do not be deterred. Keep up your personal service-excellence practice. Keep talking about the importance of focusing on service. Engage early and often. Use your band of believers to continue the conversation and keep inspiring the organization. Once you get some momentum, a lot of things will start moving on their own and begin getting infused in the DNA of a department, a division, and then, the entire company. And that's your goal. However, it will take time, and that may try your patience and drain your enthusiasm, so stay steady and be clear in your resolve. If you don't, nothing will happen, and your organization will languish in old thinking and possibly never reach its true potential.

Remember, this is a battle for the soul of your team, your department, and your organization. You must give a $#!+. You must be willing to be inconvenienced. So, like the British said during WWII, "Keep calm and carry on."

Chapter 9

Why Be Bothered?

"It is not the style of clothes one wears, neither the kind of automobile one drives, nor the amount of money one has in the bank, that counts. These mean nothing. It is simply service that measures success."
-George Washington Carver

Why should you be bothered by this? Why does this all matter? These are common questions I hear.

One word. Choice. We have choices. We have choices for where we work. We have choices for where we go to school. We have choices for who we spend our lives with. And we have choices for what we buy, as do your employees and your customers.

So how do we choose?

When it comes to products, look at the internet. You can sort by product, brand, popularity, size, reviews, newest, oldest, price, there are innumerable ways to help you make choices.

The question is, where is your business? Where is your company, your product, your work? How are customers searching? More importantly, how many customers are searching for what you do by price? If you get into that game, you are doomed, because the price game is the ticket to Commodityville. When what you do becomes about price, you are just another bag of beans. You no longer exist. Your brand, your logo, all that marketing means nothing. You have become a number.

This is why everything I have been saying is so important. Whether you are an entrepreneur, freelancer, business owner, business leader, manager, or employee down the line, you should care about this. Service is the difference maker. Remember Chapter 4 and the coffee bean/convenience store/coffee shop story? In every different option, there was a constant …coffee. The difference wasn't product; the difference was service—i.e., convenience, comfort, and removal of effort.

There are a couple of restaurants near my home and one is always busy, the other, less so. What's ironic is that the busy one has good food while the less-busy one has great food. So why is the good one so busy? Because they demonstrate giving a $#!+. They remember people, they do special things like birthday and anniversary cakes, they cater to local tastes, they just take the time to be inconvenienced by connecting with people. Put simply, they pay attention to how they do things not just what they do.

Once, I was doing some consulting for a company who was complaining about how much they were discounting their price to keep their competitors at bay. So I asked an unpopular question, one that raised eyebrows, "Why are you discounting instead of working to make price irrelevant?" You see, if your product is good but your price is perceived as too high, the quality of your service delivery is probably too low. When you provide products that get the job done and you make the experience hassle free, consistently, price begins to move out of the picture. Customers will stop sorting for price and start looking for you.

I'm not going to present a bunch of fancy statistics or extensive examples here because it's common sense. Think about the places you frequent and buy from. Do you base it all on price? When does service come into the discussion? I'll bet it is part of your thinking more than you might imagine.

Consider this. Would you prefer to go get your tires at a place that knows you, knows your car, knows your tendencies, is considerate of your budget, and every year sends you a birthday card with a coupon for an oil change, or do you go to the other shop down the street because they are a few shekels cheaper? I think I know the answer and so do you. It's simple. If you frequent businesses who have good products that do what they promise, with people who treat you well, are honest and fair, and make life easy, why do you need a raft of information to prove that your customers want the same thing?

But why is this now such a big deal? For years "*what we do*" has been enough.

It would appear we've come full circle. There was a day when every town or village had a general store where the shopkeeper knew your name, your kids' names, your parents' names, birthdays, where you lived, and what you liked. Then came industrialization with department stores and supermarkets with all that personalization being traded for greater selection. Then, when warehouse stores appeared, we traded just about any and all service for price.

But the internet and cell phones, with their speed and lack of need for brick-and-mortar locations, have changed a lot of that. Back in the days of general stores, we could get everyday products easily from someone who knew us and looked out for us. With department stores, supermarkets, and warehouse stores, we understood the tradeoffs and begrudgingly accepted the sanitized service due to the difficulties of size and scope. But now, with technology, we have the department store, supermarket, and warehouse store in our pocket. Size and scope have become irrelevant, and with that, it has given us a renewed expectation. We now want not only selection and low prices; we also want a return to that friendly, general-store care that knows us and looks out for us.

This chapter began with a question, why should you be bothered? The answer is that if you want your business to stay alive, if you want to have a job, if you want to be able to do the work you do, *what* you do is not enough; *how* you do it, how and whether you put people at the center of it—that's the difference maker. That's what will make you the choice.

Chapter 10

Final Words

"No one has ever become poor by giving."
-Anne Frank

David Blaine is a magician who has done amazing, death-defying things. He was buried alive in New York City in a coffin for a week living on nothing but water. He froze himself in a block of ice for three days and three nights. He stood on top of a one-hundred-foot pillar for 36 hours, and went to London and lived in a glass box for 44 days. He has done some seriously scary stuff and lived to tell the tale.

One day I was listening to a radio show where they were talking about fear, and in one segment, they interviewed Blaine. He said he really doesn't get scared. He said he relishes the dangerous challenges and that he is not afraid of death or injury, a trait inspired by his mother's fight with terminal illness. Then came an ironic but revealing fact. After some talk about his fearlessness and a few details about how he's been able to do the things he's done, he was asked if he had children and he said yes, a daughter. They asked if she was also fearless to which Blaine replied that his daughter was beyond fearless. "For example," he said, "she pets alligators and loves sharks." Then they asked the really telling question, "Do you ever experience the fear that a parent sometimes fears?" Before the interviewer could finish, Blaine jumped in to say, "Big time. Enormous. Even when she just, like, trips or something, I have a heart attack."

This irony immediately got me to thinking about the selflessness it demonstrated. While doing all of these death-defying stunts and not concerning himself with his own life or safety, Blaine can be worried about the tiniest thing surrounding his daughter. His thinking is set on what he can do for her and not what he can do for himself. This, as we have gone over, is the essence of giving a $#!+, and it is something that is, unfortunately, in decline.

We live in a world of increasing self-importance where laying some claim to fame has become an important pursuit. It is significant that in research on popular song lyrics there has been a dramatic increase in the use of the words I, me, and mine and a decrease in the use of the words we and us. Furthermore, a study of words used in State of the Union addresses from 1790 to 2011 show a steady increase in the use of self-interested language. While some might shrug this off as coincidence, I'm not so sure. Look at social media where people constantly post where they are, who they're with, and what they're wearing. Look at the studies on narcissism in college students that show a rise in narcissistic personality disorders. Look at the work of Christine Porath that shows a rise in incivility in the workplace. Is all of this a coincidence or is it a sad state? Well, I don't believe it's a coincidence, and yes, it is a sad state.

As we have seen, for centuries, we have been hoodwinked into believing that humans are fundamentally competitive and selfish. And while that is partially true, it is also true that we have better angels in our nature who are cooperative and helpful. However, while we listened to those better angels for the first 200,000+ years, over the last 10,000 years, we have opted more times than not for the lesser-angels option. We have warred against one another and fought viciously to win all manner of things from land to resources to wealth to the bigger slice of pie, and the fallout has been tragic. Yet, we persist. We persist in the relentless pursuit of getting more and being better than our neighbor. And nowhere has this pursuit been more relentless than our workplaces.

While every reason for business is to serve people, that has been lost and replaced with the thinking that business's prime directive is about profit, that productivity is paramount and command and control are the ways to get it, and that business, so as not to appear weak, must be void of emotion and humanity. This has left us with workplaces full of self-interest and apathy, and why customers are largely distrusting and dissatisfied. When those who serve, or are supposed to be serving, are self-focused, the experience can only be false and disappointing.

Think back to the story where we encountered a florist who had a policy that placed company interests above customer interests. It's the kind of thing most of us get from businesses on a fairly regular basis, and it sucks to be quite frank.

But it doesn't have to be this way.

In the next story, we found a few flight attendants who did things differently. They took the time to be helpful. They took the time to go out of their way to take away anxiety. They took the time to make a bad situation better and bring a little happiness to a stranger.

But why? What made them different?

Well, simply put, they gave a $#!+. They were willing to be inconvenienced by the work of compassionate service. They opened their eyes to see outside of themselves beyond their needs and their company's needs. As Daniel Goleman put it, they noticed.

But those were just a few employees, what about an organization? How can an entire organization do it?

There are all kinds of answers that people might suggest. I've even tried to do that in the preceding pages. Some are complicated and some less so, but there is fundamentally only one way to get the ball rolling and that is to build a service-focused culture, not an employee-focused or customer-focused culture, a service-focused culture.

And why? Because service is the business of business. Every business is in business to help people succeed and achieve their goals. That's it. So, if service is what business does, that should be what it focuses on and continually works to perfect.

Moreover, if you put employees or customers at the center of your attention, you inevitably exclude one or the other, but when you focus on service, you include both. When employees are well served and get what they need to be successful, they can do their best work. When customers are well served and get what they need to be successful, they can achieve their goals. So it follows, when serving is a cultural norm, everyone helps others naturally, and people see success regardless of whether they are employees or customers.

So, how does this cultural norm get created?

By communicating messages regularly and often that service is the priority. By having leaders model what it is to be of service. By encouraging cooperation and helpfulness throughout the organization. And by ensuring every delivery system is continually tweaked to show as much concern for human needs as technical ones.

But there's a rub. Until you get this service-focused foundation built, there is no point in working on things like journeys or hiring practices. And you can stop training behaviors, greetings, how to shake hands, etc. These are just bandages covering a cancer. And that cancer is having priorities in your organization's genetic makeup that compete with the fundamental purpose of helping people. It's like a sports franchise where the players are interested in personal achievement rather than winning games. Without everyone rowing together, it will never work.

But I know, you are just one person. You are one person who right now feels like I am asking you to lift the Titanic to the surface by yourself. But as I showed in Chapter 8, it's not about that; it's about developing your own practice and then, if you choose, building a following who do likewise. It's about creating a chain that gets results and influences others.

So, as I hope I have made clear, you can only do what you can do, but it does require doing something, and it begins with giving a $#!+. It begins with the willingness to be inconvenienced in the way that those flight attendants, Daniel Goleman, and even yours truly demonstrated. It begins by looking around and searching out opportunities to help those next to you, to lift them up before lifting yourself. It means seeing others as humans with needs, goals, and challenges and then adjusting what you do to be more helpful. This is where the fix begins, being willing to take the time to be aware and then taking action for someone other than yourself.

We don't have to be fearless superheroes, we just have to be willing, aware, and helpful.

So, get to work. Give a $#!+ by being willing to be inconvenienced. Make service your rally cry. Make being of service to everyone around you important. Make your bottom line caring about your work and the people it's done for. This will change everything, for you, for your workplace, and for others. And the result? A life well lived.

Go do some good!

Acknowledgements

My sincere thanks go to the following. Some have added their ideas, some were readers, some helped with editing, and still others were just influences and have supported me in some way. You have my heartfelt thanks and appreciation. In no particular order, here we go.

Geoff Bond, Ross Gimpel, Alisa Zinovoy, Jon Rennie, Greg Smith, Allister Field, Steve Foran, Eryc Eyl, Karen Cuviello, Joe Faulder, Tom North, Alexandra Fuller, Scott Walker, Nick Monks, Henry Schueller, Ed Hartshorn, Marc Mandel, Greg Boles, Scott Vengels, Nelson White, Jerry Seufert, Cynthia Brinkley Scott, Brian Scott, Sara Schairer, Leahe Murphy, Tacey Atkinson, Lason Perkins, Jeff Osterman, Stefan Ravalli, Ashley Dodge, Jeanell Greene ... and, of course, my best friend, partner, and love, Amanda Woodson.

Sources and Recommended Reading

Arbinger Institute. *The Outward Mindset*. Oakland: Berrett-Koehler Publishers, 2016.

Atkins, Paul, et al. *Prosocial*. Oakland: Context Press, 2019.

Bernshteyn, Rob. *Value as a Service*. Austin: Greenleaf Book Group, 2016.

Bregman, Rutger. *Humankind*. New York: Little, Brown and Company, 2019.

Brenner, Michael. *Mean People Suck*. West Chester: Marketing Insider Publications, 2019.

Covey, Stephen R. *The 8th Habit*. New York: Free Press, 2004.

Edmans, Alex. *Grow the Pie*. Cambridge: Cambridge University Press, 2020.

Fiske, Susan and Malone, Chris. *The Human Brand*. San Francisco: Jossey-Bass, 2013.

Freeman, R. Edward, et al. *The Power of And*. New York: Columbia University Press, 2020.

Garrett, Henry James. *This Book Will Make You Kinder*. New York: Penguin Books, 2020.

Guidara, Will. *Unreasonable Hospitality*. New York: Optimism Press, Penguin Random House, 2022.

Karlgaard, Rich. *The Soft Edge*. San Francisco: Jossey-Bass, 2014.

Klein, Stefan. *Survival of the Nicest*. New York: The Experiment, 2014.

Kohn, Alfie. *No Contest*. New York: Houghton Miflin, 1992.

Kukk, Christopher. *The Compassionate Achiever*. New York: Harper Collins, 2017.

Mazzarelli, Anthony and Trezeciak, Stephen. *Wonder Drug*. New York: St. Martin's Publishing, 2022.

Mazzarelli, Anthony and Trezeciak, Stephen. *Compassionomics*. Pensacola: Studer Group, 2019.

Meyer, Danny. *Setting the Table*. New York: Harper Collins, 2006.

Michelli, Joseph. *The New Gold Standard*. New York: McGraw-Hill, 2008.

O'Leary, Michael and Valdmanis, Warren. *Accountable*. New York: Harper Business, 2020.

Patnaik, Dev. *Wired to Care*. Upper Saddle River: FT Press, 2009.

Peters, Tom. *The Excellence Dividend*. New York: Vintage Books, 2018.

Peters, Tom. *Excellence Now: Extreme Humanism*. Chicago: Networlding Publishing, 2018

Schneider, Jakob and Stickdorn, Marc. *This is Service Design Thinking*. Hoboken: John Wiley & Sons, 2011.

Sinek, Simon. *The Infinite Game*. New York: Portfolio, Penguin Random House, 2019.

Sinek, Simon. *Leaders Eat Last*. New York: Portfolio, Penguin Random House, 2014.

Swinscoe, Adrian. *Punk CX*. Hove: Adrian Swinscoe, 2019.

About the Author

Neal Woodson is a coach, teacher, and speaker with over 20 years of experience helping people and organizations learn more about the intersection of leadership and service and how they can leverage that to create better workplace and customer life. He blogs (nealwoodson.net) and contributes regularly on LinkedIn, X, and Instagram. He is also the author of the book *The Uncomplicated Coach*, which was written for busy managers who want to increase employee engagement and improve customer experiences.

In previous lives, he worked in frontline and management roles in both the retail and restaurant industries, as a school teacher, adjunct college faculty member, AV professional in the hospitality space, and leader of training and development for a large corporation.

Currently, he and his wife live in Baltimore, MD and Edinburgh, Scotland.

To book Neal for coaching, teaching, or speaking, you can connect with him at servicecoach1@gmail.com.